IN THE SHADE

OF THE VINES

...the lovely Napa Valley lies beneath us, with its pretty farms, its majestic trees, its vineyards and orchards and farmhouses. Its villages, of which three or four were in sight, the most picturesque of which is St. Helena, are nestled among the trees at the head of the valley...an object of sublimity as well as beauty.

— Excerpt from *Up and Down California in 1860-1864*
The Journal of William H. Brewer
California State Geological Survey

In the Shade

OF THE VINES

MEADOWOOD

NAPA VALLEY

CONTENTS

FOREWORD

Agriculture has always been a source of America's great wealth, and its great pride. Yet hewing to an agricultural existence raises many difficult questions at a time when land has become one of today's most valuable commodities. Many of us in Napa Valley grapple daily with the political dilemma created by our desire for slow and sensitive growth and the preservation of our rural way of life. Implicit in our day-to-day existence are enormous issues such as economic and environmental stewardship, social and community commitment, personal visions and strong family bonds. The way in which the residents of Napa Valley respond to these compelling issues, and how they have threaded their way through them in the past, distinguishes Napa Valley from other parts of California, and of America.

It was our interest in this history—with all of its complexities and contradictions—that prompted us to think about assembling a collage of images and texts to celebrate the fortieth anniversary of Meadowood and explore its active and integral role in the life of Napa Valley as it has evolved over the years.

Life here is about evolution. Agriculture has never been a source of immediate gratification—but it does promote respect for nature, and it demands that human life adapt itself to the pace of the seasons. That is especially true when it comes to making wine: it takes a decade from the time the vineyard is first planted for it to mature and produce fruit of superior quality. Another five years may pass before people begin to enjoy the wine fully. And because some wines have a life span of twenty or thirty years, the pleasures and memories of that one particular vintage last accordingly.

Napa Valley encompasses hills and dells, mountains and valleys, creeks, ravines, and lakes. There is still forest where the land is very steep, and the oak woodlands roll down the hills into the valley floor. There are the riparian areas as well. The landscape continues to undergo the historical process of settlement, which first meant conversion from wilderness to ranchland to farmland, and later from vineyard to winegrowing estates. The story that the land tells today adds a new chapter to the continuous tale that accompanies the process of cultivating the earth. My own story echoes that same theme: I have a passion for growing grapes and making wine and working with the land—starting with the raw place and then creating something of lasting value, something that hadn't existed before.

I believe that people who grow up here, or in an environment similar to this, look at things from a perspective that implicitly comprehends that rhythmic sense of time—a perspective, I think, that's closer than most to that of our forebears. Even if Napa Valley residents are not interested in agriculture, they learn about the vagaries of working with Mother Nature. They also learn what it takes to convert those ingredients that the land provides into a product, one that is enjoyable and that can enrich the experience of life.

Those who occupy this land from San Francisco Bay to Mt. St. Helena have diverse stories, but their stories cohere into one subject around a common center. And each of these stories contributes a strand to the larger tale of the valley's culture—an epic that invests the local landscape with community pride and collective spirit. From this extraordinarily rich earth the valley's winegrowers produce one of the finest products in the world, and one of humankind's oldest. We, like the ancients, attempt to capture the seasons in a bottle—and we hope to share that with friends and family, and with the world at large.

The story of Napa Valley is foremost a story of place. This landscape is unique, and uniquely American, and as such it has played a very definite role in American history. Its geology and topography, its extraordinary subterranean riches, and its simple beauty have proved essential factors in shaping the past two centuries of existence here.

For the last half century, the wine industry has been Napa Valley's particular panorama, the grand world stage on which the local life of the valley performs. Wine combines the art of man with the bounty of nature. That endeavor weaves a web of relationships, the very relationships that make Napa Valley what it is. All the people who coexist here contribute to the valley's enterprise—not only of growing things, but also of the many activities and arts that result from wine—including the great chefs, the sommeliers, the attentive maître d's, the proprietors of fine wine shops, as well as the fire chief, the hardware store owner, the vineyard worker, and the school choir director. We agree about the need to maintain the extraordinary quality of life here and to search for the best way to shepherd this special place safely into the future. The way to do that is by nurturing its traditions, always improving and passing this culture along to future generations.

—H. William Harlan

We're farmers, first and foremost. Farming is like life: it's ongoing, you work at it, and you don't ever finish. When we finally realized that not only are things not going to be perfect, but that we can live with them that way, we began to enjoy it—but that took some time to adjust to. Of course, there are individual projects: each year you have to harvest the grapes, and make the wine, and do your marketing and sales, and everything else. It's up and down. It always will be, and you had better be ready for it.

We're both originally from southern California, and were living in San Francisco when we married in 1964. We soon began to realize that the investment business was not for Bob, and that working in an office in the city wasn't, either. One side of the family had a farming background, and we had relatives who still were farmers. Our wine hobby had been growing, and in 1967 we decided to give this a try. We found Bob a job working as a cellar rat, doing the most menial tasks. We rented a little place in Napa Valley for a year, and then bought Mayacamas Vineyards in 1968. The house dates to the 1890s, a few years after the winery was established. Think how hard it was to build a place like this, way up in the hills, with no electricity, getting the wine out on a horse cart over a dirt road. The forty years that we've been married have been incredible: when we first moved here there were only fifteen wineries, and when we traveled and people would ask us where we were from, no one had heard of Napa. Now you can say

Napa anyplace in the world, and people know.

We're all stewards of this land—we don't really own it. We hope to continue the tradition, to maintain the land, to preserve what is good and improve what needs improving. It seems to us there are other things involved in stewardship too—that it all revolves around people, finally, and taking care of each other. Stewardship is work, and life, and children, and each other. So we've been active in the Agricultural Preserve from the beginning, since around 1969. Soon after it passed, though, the restrictions started. Now farming has been outlawed in most of Napa County. You can't plant any more vineyards, anywhere. The flatland has already been planted, and it's against the law to plant on the hillsides.

We think that's a mistake. We think that the best way to preserve natural, rural life is to use the land where it's possible, because most of it is too steep, too rugged, and too rocky to be farmed anyway. What can be farmed should be farmed: this is what Napa Valley is all about. We worry about it, and it's complicated, but both of us tend to look forward more than backward. We don't have much time to reflect, so we try to make the best of what we're doing. It's like being a great Olympic sprinter: don't look back because the runner behind may be gaining on you.

—Bob and Nonie Travers

The land is not the setting for the work but a part of the work.

Walter De Maria, Artist

THE NIGHT AUDITOR

My dad worked for the Pullman Railroad doing the inlaid woodwork for the car interiors—his fingers were stubbier and bigger than mine, and how he could do inlay work I never could comprehend. Yet I saw him do it, and I have a cedar chest that he made for me out of the wood used for Pullman Railroad cars. It's beautiful!

I was born in Chicago in 1932. Our neighborhood was called Roseland: it was on the far south side of town, and at that time it wasn't uncommon to find a different nationality every six or eight blocks.

We played ball right in the streets. We set our bases out along the curbs and played ball. We weren't very far from Cicero, Illinois, where Al Capone had his dynasty. I can recall that we'd all go for a drive on a Sunday afternoon, and my dad would make a point of going through there to show us where this famous, or infamous, guy hung out.

My dad retired about the time that I finished grade school. At that time we moved to a rural community in southwestern Michigan, between Grand Rapids and Kalamazoo, where my father bought a small farm. I was just fourteen at the time. We lived ten miles from the nearest high school, Allegan High School, which meant walking a mile and a half to the corner for the school bus.

In the summer they showed movies in a little country schoolhouse near where I lived. I saw this good-looking blonde girl there, and happily, I had to walk right past her home to get to the shows. Joyce and I went together until we got married in the summer of 1953.

She was my high school sweetheart, and we've been married for fifty years now! She's the love of my life. We had our fiftieth anniversary at Meadowood, in the Wine Library. It was fine, very fine, but I got above my gums, and I even cried a little—and I don't cry easily.

After high school I enlisted in the Air Force. I was nineteen, and the draft was on for the Korean War. When I got there, they asked me, what do you want to be—a cook or a clerk? Well, I didn't want to cook, and because I'm an administrative, numbers-type of person, I ended up in office work. I served for four years.

My first job was with Wilson Sporting Goods, stamping the heads of Walter Hagen golf clubs—I walked his dog a few times, and shook his hand many times. In January of 1964, Wilson moved me to San Francisco. Coincidentally, Wilson used to supply a young tennis star named Doug King, the tennis pro here at Meadowood, when he was a student down in, I believe it was, Walnut Creek, California. We used to provide him with racquets and balls and various other tennis gear.

I like my job as the night auditor here at Meadowood because, for one, it's a numbers thing. It helps me to evaluate how things are going. Of course, I don't see the actual flow of people or the things that they do and don't do because I work the night shift, but it makes it easier for me to sense the things that I see.

As life goes on, you do learn about a lot of things. One thing I've learned over the years is to talk about things rather than being grumpy about them. I like to think that I'm a tenderhearted person.

—Len Dowiat

THE LIFE OF THE BEE

Let us go on, then, with the story of our hive; let us take it up where we left it; and raise, as high as we may, a fold of the festooned curtain in whose midst a strange sweat, white as snow and airier than the down of a wing, is beginning to break over the swarm. For the wax that is now being born is not like the wax that we know; it is immaculate, it has no weight; seeming truly to be the soul of the honey, that itself is the spirit of flowers. And this motionless incantation has called it forth that it may serve us, later—in memory of its origin, doubtless, wherein it is one with the azure sky, and heavy with perfumes of magnificence and purity—as the fragrant light of the last of our altars.

— Maurice Maeterlinck, excerpt from *The Life of the Bee*

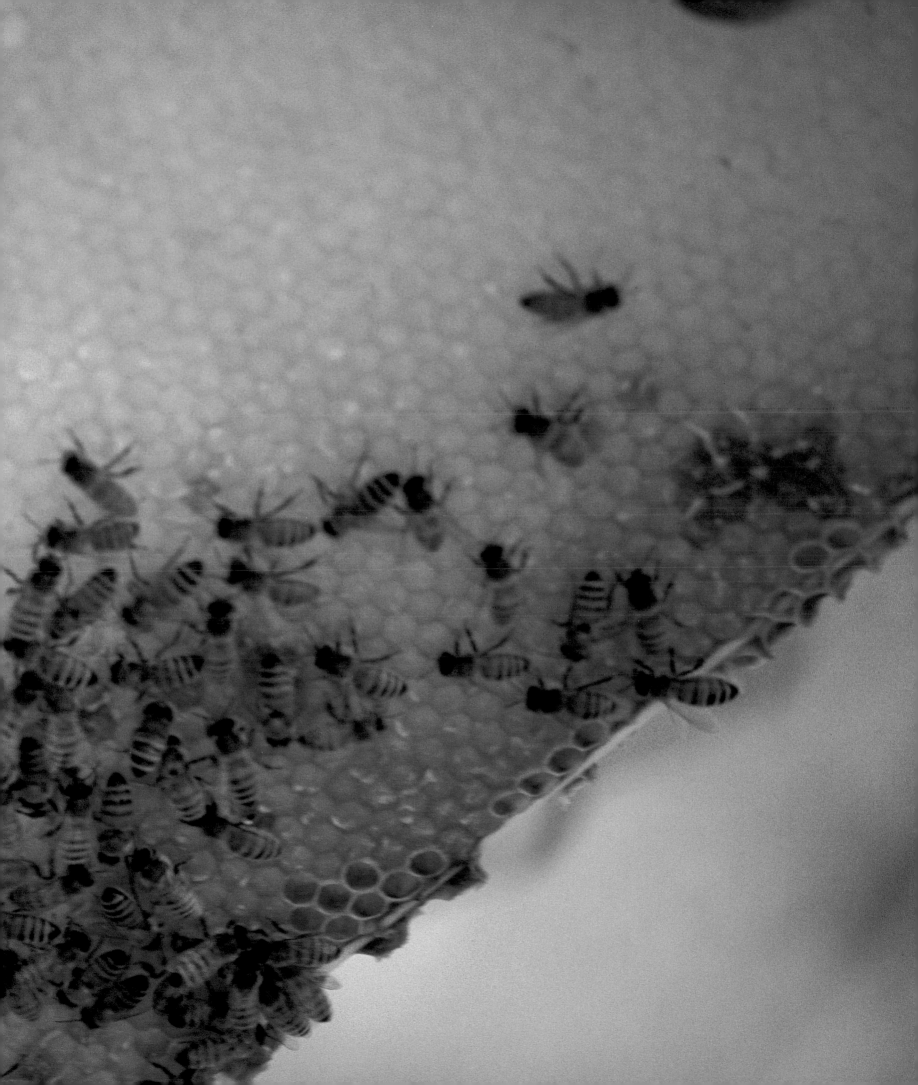

I

Gathering

ROSALIA DAVALOS

To me, family is just a magic word. It means being united, being together, and loving each other, and helping each other. Whenever we have family gatherings, it's great because there are usually twenty people or thirty people, just with the family—brothers, sisters, my nephews, nieces. It's just pretty much being together, you know, and loving each other, helping each other.

Being one of the youngest of seven has made me more eager to succeed. It's been a challenge most of my life—not trying to compete, but trying to be at the same level as my older brothers and sisters. My mom did a good job at that, teaching us to be independent. We try to help each other, but we all do different things.

In Mexico, I ran cross-country—that's what I loved the most. All my brothers used to play soccer, and I played with them—running with boys, playing a lot of sports. But I liked running the best.

We moved here because of my dad, who used to work here picking grapes in the hillside vineyards for about twenty years. In my early childhood, my dad was gone a good part of the time. He would come to Mexico every year, usually in December for Christmas, for about three months.

Coming from Michoacan in 1993 was a big transition. My father moved all my older brothers first. My little brother, my mom, and me were the last ones to come into the country, but we were all together for the first time in a long time.

I started learning English when I came here, and in high school that's what I mostly studied. I also used to tutor Americans for the Spanish classes. There was this teacher, Mrs. Ellington—I didn't like her then, but she made a difference in my life. She had a Hispanic literature class; it was actually called Chicano literature class. We learned a lot about different cultures, about different writers that I didn't know—good writers, Hispanic-American writers. It was a good class, and I really got to express a lot of my feelings in that class. I had her for my English as a Second Language classes too, so I had her for a good three years and I loved it.

I remember one of the things that I didn't like—and I would always cry—was when we would give speeches to the class about the transition, about moving to this country. I don't know why, but I remember I would cry when I would start speaking about that. I was already getting used to this place, but I felt like I would remember growing up in Mexico and my past there. Obviously we didn't have all the things that kids have growing up here. I guess I missed being in Mexico, but at the same time I felt lucky and happy to be here. And that's one of the reasons I used to cry—because I just felt lucky to be here, to be learning, and to be seeing all the doors opening for me. I got so nervous speaking in front of that class.

I don't cry about memories of Mexico anymore. We visit for the holidays and then we come back here. This is home for us now.

—Rosalia Davalos

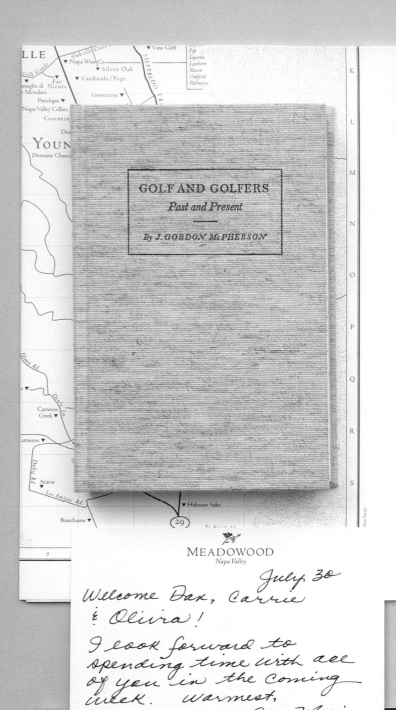

GOLF AND GOLFERS
Past and Present
—
By J. GORDON McPHERSON

YOUN...

Croquet

🌿
MEADOWOOD
Napa Valley

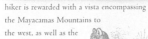
MADAMA BUTTERFLY
(da JOHN L. LONG e DAVID BELASCO) — TRAGEDIA GIAPPONESE
DI L·ILLICA E G·GIACOSA · MUSICA DI
GIACOMO PUCCINI
G·RICORDI & C·EDITORI

🍇
MEADOWOOD
Napa Valley

July 30
Welcome Dax, Carrie
& Olivia!
I look forward to
spending time with all
of you in the coming
week. Warmest,
Ann Marie

900 MEADOWOOD LANE • ST. HELENA, CALIFORNIA 94574 • TEL. (707) 963-1646

🍇
MEADOWOOD
Napa Valley

THE Meadowood Trail offers a fascinating glimpse into the Napa Valley's unique ecosystem. A quick hike demonstrates the rugged natural beauty that becomes a part of all who know and love Meadowood, and offers panoramic vistas into the larger Valley beyond.

WINDING through Pacific woodland forest and mountain chapparal, the challenging eastern sections of the Meadowood Trail rise quickly to a height of over 600 feet. In the lower sections, alder, oak, and manzanita predominate, with the occasional giant Douglas Fir, towering above.

MULE DEER

...of deer, ra... ...re commo... ...ors are wa... ...nakes and ...ions, thoug... ...ntered, ...nd their ... ...should be... ...the utmost respect.

...t the crest of the trail's ascent the hiker is rewarded with a vista encompassing the Mayacamas Mountains to the west, as well as the city of St. Helena, many hillside and valley vineyards, and other recognizable local landmarks.

As the trail descends ... property, the terrain be... western portion offer ... under the canopy of o... you choose to roam or ... please stay on the trails... residents (whether anim... and have a great hike!

MOUNTAIN LION

BOUCHON

4534 Washington St., Yountville, CA 94599, tel (707) 944-8037, fax (707) 944-2769

Philippe Jeanty
PÈRE JEANTY
BISTRO PROVENÇAL
6725 WASHINGTON STREET YOUNTVILLE, CA 94599
PHONE (707) 945-1000 • FAX (707) 945-1100
VISIT US AT WWW.PEREJEANTY.COM

NEST
CAFE • TAKEOUT • CATERING
Kate & Mardi Schma   7787 St. Helena Hwy.
707•944•0206   Napa, CA 94562

OAKVILLE
GROCERY®

MARY DANIELAK
Corporate Wine Buyer
Oakville Grocery Company, Inc.
7856 St. Helena Highway
Oakville, CA 94562
Tel: 707-944-8802
Fax: 707-944-1844
mdanielak@oakvillegrocery.com

DEAN &
MAI...
607 SOUTH ST HELENA...
707 967 988...

Dear Mr. Miller —
What a pleasure to have you
forever join us for dinner on
Wednesday.

I hope we met your
expectations and look forward to

AGED FOR 20 YEARS
IN THE NAPA VALLEY

St. Helena Calif. (Father)

1942 RANCH Silverado Trail St. Helena Calif.

THE
MEADOWOOD
TRAIL

| MEADOWOOD TRAILS | |
Hiking Distances	
Head to Lower Overlook	.4 miles
Head to Viewpoint	.8 miles
Head to Valley Viewpoint	1.0 miles
D. Trail Head to Golf Course	1.2 Miles
E. Trail Head to Lakeside	1.4 miles
Meadowood Loop Trail Head to Trail Head	1.6 miles

(All distances are measured from the Trail Head)

Roads	Unpaved Roads
Hiking Trails	Pathways
▼ Trail Head	⬛ Steep
● Trail Marker	⬛ Parking

Please
do not walk on
the Golf Course

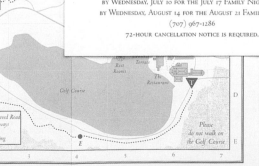

1938 St. Helena Calif. (Mother)

VISITING A FRIEND'S COUNTRY ESTATE

Though I had never been there before, I recognized the place immediately. From the approach through the mouth of the valley within the greater valley where it sits, along a narrow lane edged by a vineyard and flower-drenched stone walls, it resonated with something inexplicably familiar. A two-hundred-year-old oak *allée*—stretching outward from an antebellum house in Virginia—once had the same effect on me. The sensation lives in an elusive marriage of details, behind a hedgerow, around a column, underneath an archway, in a weather-beaten folly or a recluse's walled garden or on an entire ancestral estate six generations removed from its builder. Charm is far too simple a word, though those things do possess fantastic charm. This is something older and less accessible, a kind of longing and a desire for belonging and ownership. Once, I was shown a ruined sugar mill hidden in a dell surrounded by cane fields on Maui, its rusted steel beams and tall brick walls encased within the trunk of a huge banyan tree; I experienced the same sensation next to the stacked folios, Freud portraits, and tattered upholstery in the Duke of Devonshire's library at Chatsworth. Impossible to fake, the phenomenon is rare and precious, an enchantment one part plan and two parts accident, loaded with meaning and memory.

A few people in the world understand the universal principles of comfort intrinsically and can produce them with little difficulty.

A hostess I knew in England had her footmen put the toothpaste on your toothbrush while you were downstairs at dinner, and her housemaids slip into your bedroom at dawn to light a fire in the grate. Another, in New England, expected you to bring your own sheets and at least one delicacy—a prosciutto, a hunk of cheddar, a bottle of olive oil—for a quixotic and unpredictable Saturday night dinner. There was minimal heat in this weekend house and it was dead winter, but what I really remember about visiting her—other than sleeping in my clothes because I forgot sheets—were the other guests and how they jumped into conversation and after-dinner games.

I arrived for my visit at dusk in early autumn, the air thick with ripe grapes for my passage through Napa Valley to the outskirts of St. Helena. I was shown to my room and brought a supper of grilled salmon. The cottage had a rural grace, its ceiling high and white with the cross-hatching of the roof beams left exposed like a camp in the Adirondacks. Walls were clad in an old-fashioned everyday bead-board paneling like so many summer houses; a span of windows wrapped around three sides. At the foot of my bed was a sofa facing an enormous fireplace.

This room reflected a trait characteristic of all the buildings on the estate and, I gathered, of its patrons' manners: a slightly tempered formality, a sturdy earthiness rounded out with refinement. French doors, bronze railings, doorknobs and hinges—solid, quality—pediments over doorways and dormer windows signed with an eccentric arced base, ennobled buildings sheathed, conversely, in clapboard, the most common siding in the American vernacular. ("It combined in an easy perfection the charms of civilization and nature" is how Lord David Cecil, the historian and critic, explained the same ideal as expressed by the English aristocracy of the eighteenth century.)

The estate borrows a few of the symbols and traditions of stately permanence from old Eastern establishments; however, the ties and collars have been loosened and the riding boots pulled off. There is an emphasis on polite society—that is, if you are interested—or, if you prefer, an equal emphasis on privacy. Someone from the staff is there if you want, not if you don't, the same with the other guests.

Lichen suffuses the garden walls, stepping-stones, and massive tree trunks; vines shroud court fences; great shocks of white iceberg roses shoot out of pots by the pool and from stray corners. All over the grounds I found secret pauses in the flow of life: a bench, a shaded perch, a table with an umbrella and an exquisite lunch.

If I hadn't been hobbled by a sporting accident, games would have been a part of my stay. Instead, I looked on the golf course and croquet lawn more as clever features in an architect's bag of tricks rather than as places to play. From this perspective I understood all the qualities that so distinguish a good "natural landscape," or *jardin anglais,* and the magical way it can affect a man's serenity; bewitching contrasts and contradictions made tacit in the decisive angles of a croquet lawn give way to the organic forms that shape the tees, sand traps, and greens of a nine-hole golf course, and that then slip away altogether into the ecstatic flora and fauna around the valley's brim. This apt metaphor for the people and place is carved out of the very ground itself. The signs say that proper whites are required when playing croquet. Apparently at one time there were rice paddies on the floor of this small valley where there are now fairways. I relished this perspective from my dinner table. The seductive pull of a wide swath of green vanishes elusively behind a spinney or over a copse.

I met one of the valley's vintners, and he invited me on a tour of his own estate. I saw from his library that he was a reader of architectural monographs, and learned that he studied how to make his celebrated wine in France from the old-school masters. His many acres of trussed-up vines—hugging the slopes and dips of a Napa hillside—resembled the grooves in a perfectly combed head of slicked hair, and the house he built above his fields sat on exactly the right rise, just where someone like him from another epoch might have put a house centuries ago or will centuries from now. He was good company, and there was a glimmer in his eye when he spoke of his wine and what he was creating for his children's children, of the high standards he tries to keep, and of plans for stemming the flood tide of development from ruining the valley. ("Theirs was not an unreal life, no Watteau-like paradise of exquisite trifling and fastidious idleness," wrote Cecil. "For one thing it had its roots in the soil.") I counted three kitchens on his estate, but my guess is there are closer to eight; he reveres hospitality and living by the seasons, eating what a fertile kitchen garden can produce.

Evocative remnants—the foundation and the engraving—are as powerful as any sonata or dirge. Once, there was a fantastic retreat on the island of Huahine near Tahiti. Everything on the breathtaking, ocean-side site was conceived and designed by one driven man. He oversaw its meticulous construction as well. Each of the guesthouses and resort buildings was unique; the bar, for instance, was made in a fluid shape suggestive of an enormous fish, and the dining pavilion was a great thatch-covered abstraction, worthy of Eero Saarinen, with walls made of translucent shells. This magician created canopied staircases to snake the property's volcanic hills, and had a hand in most of the elegant furniture and bathroom fixtures there, even the still lifes made fresh every morning from papaya and palm fronds. A few years ago a cyclone hit the island and in one short moment completely razed this man's twenty-year-old testament to longing, leaving behind a few lava-rock idols and a junk-filled swimming pool. Now Hina Iti's ruin is a monument. These places and societies keep popping up on the landscape like wild mushrooms, only to disappear into history. Some, those with deeper roots, last a little longer than the others. There are marvelous people who envision these places for themselves, and sometimes for others who want to join them. This is perhaps why this place in Napa Valley, an ideal of stone and collective nostalgia, seemed so familiar to me. I had been there before.

—Robert Becker

2

Sanctuary

THIS MEADOW
AND THESE WOODS

This is a private realm, by nature and by design, yet it harbors discoveries more than secrets, equally gracious to those who know it as to those welcomed for the first time. Enter the small valley through the oak and laurel tunnel and follow the low wall of volcanic rock, porous stone that holds the weight of history—and it is here the senses awaken and the body lightens. Discreet clapboard cottages cluster on tiptoe across the eastern hillside, each with its own perspective and a distinct address: the first just up from the pool, under the low branch of a redwood, the last at the top of a trail with a view over the tops of the fir and pine trees. Every porch and stair landing and window seat is an intention, an invitation to pause, to rest, to wonder. Inside the cottages, each one generous with simple luxuries, calmness reigns and comfort cushions. Slivers of sun glint off nickel-plated taps and dart through beams under lofty whitewashed ceilings. Big windowpanes silently frame nature as art.

At close range, textures become distinguishable, fragrances distinct, tones traceable to their sources. You are as alone as you want to be—or not to be. The shriek of soles and thwocking of balls ricochets from tennis court to hill to dale. Whoops follow, answered by gleeful splashes from the family pool.

It's the song of release and delight, the discovery of hive and haven in one. Sound shifts with the sun, but mostly it keeps to the valley

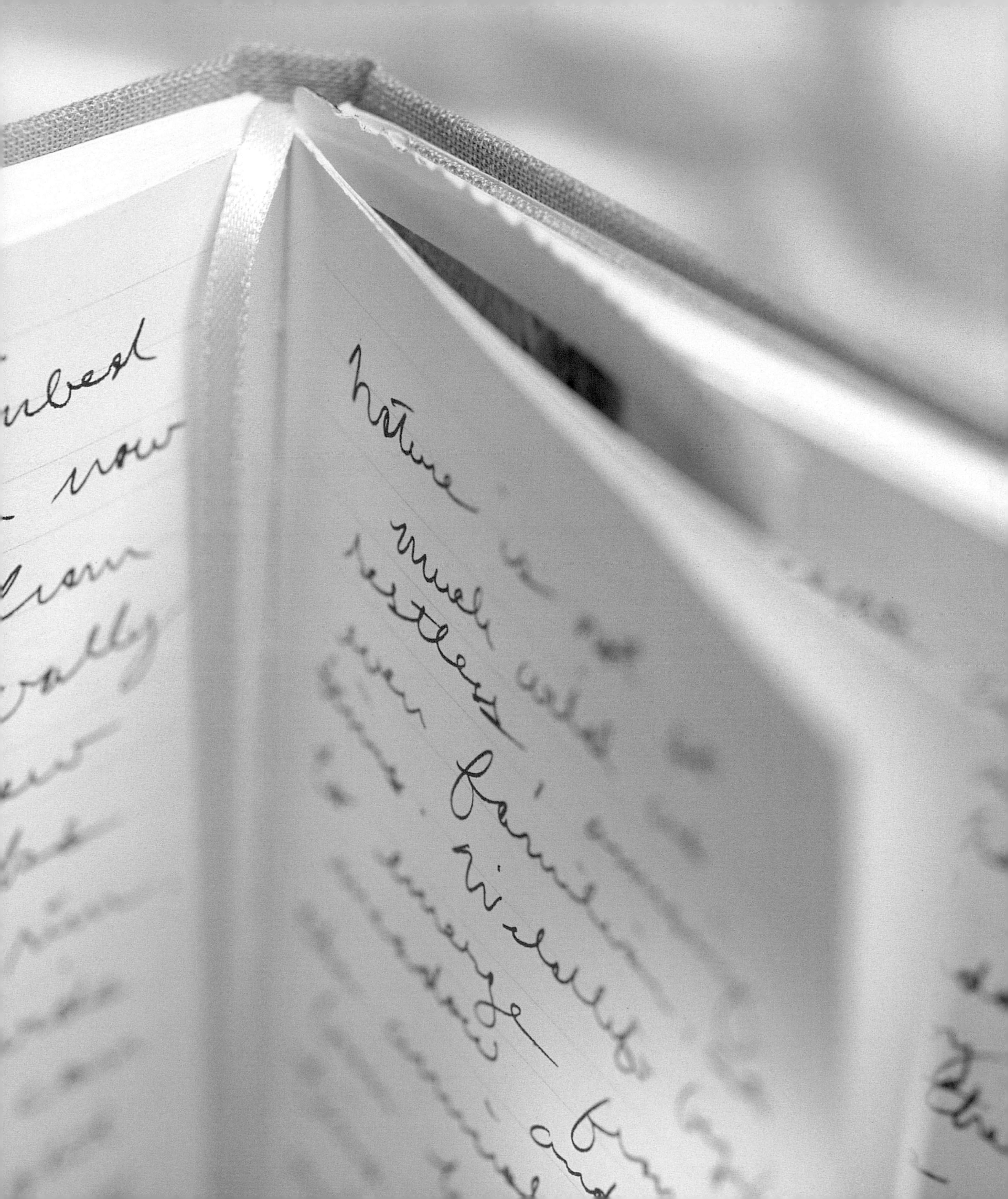

floor, trickling down from the hillside cottages to gather at nests of nourishment and community—the lodge, the restaurant, the health spa. There is yoga at noon with an instructor who endows you with new suppleness and a share of her own natural grace. You stretch in silence but for deliberate breaths. Warmth comes from within. Hold the pose, shift, reach, breathe—slow, slower, even slower—until meditation is simply a natural state.

At the spa one treatment involves the laying on of four hands and smooth stones, first pumice hot as coals, then marble cold as ice. The stones glide and press on oiled skin guided by silent fingers. The muscles grimace, then smile, and cheeks turn to roses. You are tuned to a different frequency now, intoxicated by the scent of rosemary from a hedge, mesmerized by hummingbirds spinning around feeders near the spa deck, and at your slower pulse their speed is that much more dazzling. Your eyes can no more keep up with their wings than their wings can match the desire of their bills. Nectar, the sound of the word sticks in the throat, so thick and sweet. Yet the birds drink deeply and still flit and dance like sparks—fitting for wine country.

Nature is not so much wild as restless, amusing, even familiar, at times. Wildlife begins to emerge from the meadow and woods: the animals have been here all along, but you've only just begun to notice. A pair of lizards skitter along rough boulders that border the croquet lawns, pausing for brisk push-ups and a quick tête-à-tête before rushing on. A dark-eyed junco appears to fall from the sky, tucking then spreading its wings, in-out, in-out, to brake its steep swoop.

A trail runs along the perimeter of this meadow, with tangents and

byways that climb the slopes and descend into the woods. It is both escape and arrival, beautiful and alive. At first the going is steep, but each pause is a window. You are greeted by manzanita bushes, their claret branches like coral, and by one-hundred-year-old pines rocketing upward, centenarians standing watch.

You have climbed high enough to emerge from this secret valley and gain the view of the hawks that trace its rim. The sky is wide now. You can see fog caught by the ridge of the Mayacamas off to the west. As the sun skips between clouds, it exposes first a patch of vineyard far below, then turns a stand of fir from deep emerald to chartreuse. Repose is beneath, around, above, and especially within. It is here, where the ping of air particles is felt, where subtle sound travels alongside seductive scent, where light constantly shifts and dances, that sanctuary lies.

—Heather McIsaac

CROQUET

ELLERY McCLATCHY: If you're into croquet, it changes your life. It takes time, and because it takes time, the people you see are croquet players, so you socialize with them a lot. We don't know how or why you get the passion, and someone else at the same time doing the same thing—who looks like a friend—he doesn't get it.

Jerry fell in love with the game. It happened to me, too, and I don't know why. I wasn't an athlete as a child. I did ski, but I had a very bad accident in my mid-twenties and I was restricted as to what I could do after that. But I could play croquet, and I can still play it. I fooled around with the backyard version for a number of years. And then I went to a croquet match in Central Park. The competition was held on the course, the green, there—a regular croquet green. And I fell in love with it. When I went back to my place in the country, I bulldozed my koi, that pond, which wasn't working, and packed it with sand and dirt, and planted it with sod. In three months I was playing on it. It wasn't very good, though, so then I took the time and I chopped away a mountainside and put in a full court, which was first-class.

JERRY STARK: I played croquet in the backyard as a kid, too. In high school I played football and basketball and ran track, and I've played golf since I was eight years old. But like Ellery, I fell for Association Croquet the first time I played it. Almost immediately after I played that first game of Association Croquet, I picked up and moved from Kansas City to Phoenix so I could play more. I was dating the woman I later married, and I had a few jobs—and I moved anyway.

The relationship that Ellery and I have started in Arizona, at the first Arizona Open, a very important, early croquet tournament held in 1983. After play one day, on the second or third day of the tournament, I was introduced to him. Everyone was heading off to dinner. I'd only been in Phoenix about a month, but I knew where we were going to dinner. Ellery didn't know, or he needed a ride—I can't remember which. So I drove him to dinner to meet everybody else, or he drove me. And we talked and got to know each other. Then I saw him in Florida at a tournament. When I moved out here we played more, and Ellery started his tournament, which I run for him. We share our courts for a couple of tournaments each year.

ELLERY: Croquet can be very social and it can be very seriously competitive, as Jerry knows. My tournament is more of a social tournament than a serious, world-championship-type tournament—except that top players are there. They're definitely competitive when they play their game. But afterwards we have nice visits, and even families get together.

JERRY: When I'm playing Ellery—no, not with him, because he knows the game too well—but if I'm playing someone who looks like he's making an error, I talk to him. We help each other out. When I'm playing in the World Championships it's totally serious, but it's a lot more social here. Although just stepping inside that string, the croquet gods put on that switch of competitiveness—for anybody who steps inside that string.

ELLERY: Most people play croquet just on the weekends, like weekend golfers. Croquet has been an integral part of my life, though,

68

and it's an integral part of Jerry's life. It can be a great, fun game as played at all levels. I play it socially. And Jerry sometimes plays it socially. If anything, you see Jerry going around on the croquet court making very delicate, handsome shots. He's got the touch. The American game, it's a touch game, because you want to hit balls and not hit them over the line if they're close to the line. You can laugh and enjoy, but I remember one time when Jerry was playing at my tournament and there was someone who was beating him—and he went off and sat by himself. He just sat by himself, like a lion, a dejected lion, while he was watching what the other guy had done to him.

Croquet is a reflective sport. It gives you time to get nervous, or to figure things out and decide what to do. It's like any other sport in that judgment matters, judgment and skill.

JERRY: But croquet is a game that ordinarily is not played with referees. If you and I are playing a game of croquet, we're the referees of the game. You only call a referee when, between the two of you, you can't decide something. You're on an honor system, a total honor system. Croquet ethics are one of the first things you learn. But you can also be vicious.

ELLERY: It's a very polite game and you say nice things, but you're thinking and doing terrible things to the opposition. Like chess, there are openings, tactics that everybody knows about. Croquet can be one of the most stressful games there is.

When the olive tree first came to Alta California, it came in serious company. Along with the pomegranate, the fig and the vine, the Franciscans brought it from the older mission gardens of Baja California, in 1769 or soon after. In slowness of growth, in legend of life, in grace and dignity, it remains a tree of legend.

—Hildegarde Flanner, excerpt from
At the Gentle Mercy of Plants

3

A Brief History of Napa Valley

To the Members of the
Vintners association of the Napa Valley

Dear Friends,

At my last monthly luncheon of
your association at Meadowood, I was
offered several magnums a beautiful
gift very much appreciated.

Then at the 1994 Wine auction
under the Tent another wonderful gift
an "Imperial" bottle (Mathusalem in champagne) of Sterling 1987. All these wines
graciously sent to my home in France.

To drink that huge bottle I had
to wait for a great Celebration with
many guests. It came on July 4th of
this year our golden Wedding anniversary
(yes you gain your independence on that day
I lost mine)

The wine was absolutely beautiful
and very well received by all present.

It was also the occasion to raise
our glasses to ... great ...

Many ...

Enclose...

day. I am with my son Patrick
(some of you know him) he is now
Resident Manager of the Cipriani hotel
in Venice. Should some of you go
to that beautiful City he'll be delighted to see you.

Fond memories remain of my
eight years in the Napa Valley
Best Wishes to all of you
Sincerely
Maurice Nayrolles.

Mme et Mr Maurice NAYROLLES
11 Parc Vigier
23 Bld Franck Pilatte
06300 NICE

PRIORITAIRE
PRIORITY

Mr Mrs H. W. Harlan
P.O Box 365
OAKSVILLE CA. 94562

U.S.A.

To the Members of the Vintners Association of the Napa Valley

Dear Friends,

At my last monthly luncheon of your association at Meadowood, I was offered several magnums, a beautiful gift very much appreciated.

Then at the 1994 Wine auction under the tent another wonderful gift an "Imperial" bottle (Methusalem in champagne) of Sterling 1987. All these wines graciously sent to my home in France.

To drink that huge bottle I had to wait for a great celebration with many guests. It came on July 4th of this year our golden wedding anniversary (yes you gain your independence on that day I lost mine).

The wine was absolutely beautiful and was very well received by all present.

It was also the occasion to raise our glasses to your great nation.

Many many thanks again.

Enclosed is the photo taken that day. I am with my son Patrick (some of you know him) he is now Resident Manager of the Cipriani hotel in Venice. Should some of you go to that beautiful city he'll be delighted to see you.

Fond memories remain of my eight years in the Napa Valley.

Best wishes to all of you.

Sincerely

Maurice E Nayrolles

2000 B.C. – 1830s   1823   1833

This land was once their land, from California to the New York islands. During the thousands of years when Mt. St. Helena was called kana'mota, or human mountain, the Patwin and Wappo Indians (from guapo, meaning brave) settled villages and farmed the good earth of Napa Valley. This peaceful tribe descended from the valley's earliest inhabitants (an occupation dating back thousands of years). The Wappo were initially hospitable to the explorers of Alta California—but not for long. By 1835, decimated by a smallpox epidemic, they began battling the settlers claiming vast tracts of land for cultivation and cattle grazing. Ultimately, they surrendered, only to experience displacement, disease, and degradation. An ever-dwindling population of Wappo camped around the European settlements for the next half century until, eventually, the Wappo culture and even the language were lost.

Spanish missions provide the last visible traces of the intrepid friars who colonized the new world from Mexico to Alta California three centuries ago. Father Jose Altamira, a Spanish priest, was the first European to explore Napa Valley, Carneros, and Sonoma. He also noted, presciently, that the area was "proper for the cultivation of grapes." San Francisco de Solano, above, built in 1823, was the northern terminus of the Spanish Empire in the Americas. It was the last mission completed prior to Mexico's successful push for independence. The missions were subsequently secularized in 1833. Sonoma's town square now occupies the site of the Solano mission, which once controlled 700 square miles—including the Napa Valley.

Social Darwinism may be a twentieth-century concept, but it has always been a political principle: the fittest do survive. Take Mariano Vallejo, for example. This Mexican aristocrat was named general and commander of Mexico's Northern Frontier, controlling hundreds of thousands of acres no longer under Spanish dominion. During the "land grab" of the early 19th century, Vallejo established a presidio in Santa Rosa, parceling out property and accelerating population growth in Mexico's new territory. He handed over land liberally to those who agreed to adopt both Mexican citizenship and Catholicism, and, fulfilling both conditions himself, personally claimed almost a quarter of a million prime Sonoma acres. The barely bilingual Vallejo became one of California's first elected officials, winning the race for state senator in 1849.

1836   1840   1841

George Calvert Yount, the mountaineer who in 1836 was the first American settler in the Napa Valley, once claimed to see sixty bears in a single day. As historian Lin Weber noted, "In 1843, being mauled by a bear in the Napa Valley was a much greater risk than being attacked by a hostile native." General Vallejo—impressed by Yount's carpentry skills and, apparently, his work ethic—employed him. Vallejo later renamed the North Carolinian Jorge and granted him 12,000 acres in the middle of what was then Wappo country (the area now encompassing Yountville, Oakville, and Rutherford), which Yount named Rancho Caymus. Yount later planted grape cuttings purchased from General Vallejo; in 1854 he hosted a wine tasting for regional journalists. Those published comments, which, prophetically, made comparisons to Bordeaux, are among the earliest recorded impressions of Napa wines.

As Rodgers and Hammerstein so memorably put it, "The farmer and the cowman should be friends." In nineteenth-century California, they were. Territory folks imported thousands of cattle, making ranching Napa Valley's primary industry. Some members of the dwindling Native American population became vaqueros; others continued to attack arriving settlers. As Manifest Destiny impelled people west, Napa Valley welcomed more white settlers than anywhere in California except San Francisco. Farming soon joined ranching as the region's leading enterprise. Wheat was the valley's principal crop until the 1870s, when drought and declining prices caused farmers to plant grapes and orchards of peaches, pears, and apples.

Dr. Edward Turner Bale, an English surgeon with a nasty temper who married one of General Mariano Vallejo's many nieces, Maria Soberanes, was granted a tract of land in 1841 that he named Rancho Carne Humana. The notoriously hotheaded Bale was almost lynched in Sonoma for shooting General Vallejo's brother Salvador after being bested by Salvador's sword in a duel. Bale initiated the duel by tossing down a particularly heinous gauntlet—accusing Señor Vallejo of a romantic and incestuous dalliance with Bale's wife. Frontier justice decided the brouhaha was merely a family dispute, so Bale stayed out of prison. In 1846, Bale built the area's first gristmill, then something of a local hangout, now a state landmark and Napa County's oldest surviving structure.

1846   1848   1849

President James Polk announced his intention to annex California, so infuriating Mexico that the recently independent country threatened war. Some California settlers took Polk's desire to heart, and matters into their own hands, arresting General Vallejo at his Sonoma home in June of 1846 and declaring that the Mexican territory under Vallejo's aegis was henceforth (at least for the next sixty days) the "California Republic." The rebels hailed their quasi-state with a makeshift flag—a star and a grizzly bear— thus the Bear Flag Rebellion. Peter Storm, a celebrated Bear Flagger, above, carried what he claimed was the true Bear Flag, hoisting it in Napa Valley parades for several decades. Mexico and the United States declared war in July of 1846; by the following year, the U.S. had appropriated the California territory—statehood followed shortly thereafter.

Captain John Sutter discovered he had the Midas touch and was going to be as rich as Croesus by chance. Workers, digging a channel on his property at Coloma, in the foothills of the Sierra Nevada, spied a gleam in the river. In one of history's more propitious coincidences, the revelation of Sutter's gold followed by a mere nine days the declaration of peace between Mexico and America. "There's gold in them thar hills!" became a rallying cry for countless adventurers around the globe: what had been a trickle of humanity flowing ever westward became a flood of prospectors rushing headlong into California. Many of the first arrivals found their pots of gold in the rivers at the base of the Sierras, including American soldiers sent to California to fight in the Mexican- American War and struggling pioneers settling the Napa Valley.

Sam Brannan, a classic American show-man (though perhaps not of the same ilk as the über-marketer, P. T. Barnum), marched through the streets of San Francisco waving a bag of gold dust, generating public hysteria and fueling the gold rush. Brannan set up shop near Sutter's Claim, selling mining supplies at grossly inflated prices to the thousands of prospectors swarming the area. The gold rush made him a rich man: in 1860 he spent a small fortune, more than $500,000, building Calistoga's Hot Springs Hotel and promoting the town as a playground for the crème de la crème of San Francisco society. Brannan's Calistoga folly succeeded, but his resort never attracted the elite crowd he sought. Brannan had arrived on a ship carrying Mormon settlers to Yerba Buena in 1846—the city was renamed San Francisco the next year.

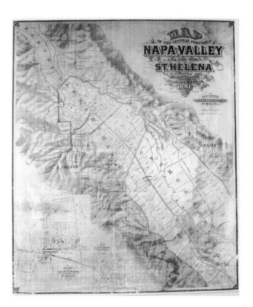

1852   1853   1854

Getting away from it all is not a new idea, but it's one that California's settlers were quick to realize. White Sulphur Springs, the state's first resort, opened in 1852, near what was soon to become the town of St. Helena. This venture was not an instant hit. It changed hands several times and burned to the ground twice before Sven Alstrom, an experienced hotelier, purchased it. By 1861, however, the professionally hospitable Swede had turned it into a renowned vacation destination. As historian Lin Weber wrote, "Guests often came with their servants, their linen, and their own china and were treated like royalty....Quite a few of the guests were so taken by this that they eventually bought land nearby and put in vineyards." White Sulphur Springs championed the modern conveniences necessary for its guests' comfort: St. Helena's first phone line linked the resort to the San Francisco stock exchange.

By 1853, settlers began cutting the roads that they and their heirs would use to cultivate community from the wilderness. One of these early byways ran from St. Helena up Howell Mountain Road (named for the blacksmith who helped to forge St. Helena's future) through Angwin, down into Pope Valley and north into Lake County, providing access through what had once been General Vallejo's thousands of acres, including the property he had given to his niece, Maria Soberanes. Her holdings contained the land at the junction of the Silverado Trail and Howell Mountain Road, which, uniquely, encompassed forest, woodland, grassland, and the riparian area down to the Napa river (pictured above).

St. Helena was founded in 1854. It began to blossom, with a blacksmith shop, a wagon and carriage depot, and a small hotel opening along Main Street by 1856. Napa, settled in 1846, and Yountville, established in 1855, rounded out the valley's first three towns. By 1852, Napa had 2,116 residents, only 252 of them women; by the middle of that decade there was evidence of a maturing community with an opera house, a lyceum, crowded hotels, and teeming saloons. St. Helena continued to grow in a suburban mold, according to William H. Brewer, who visited in 1861: "St. Helena, with its fifty or more houses, many of them neat and white, nestled among grand old oaks, was very picturesque." Over the next few decades, the pretty village in the valley absorbed waves of immigrants from Germany and the Mississippi Valley, wealthy San Franciscans, and Chinese laborers.

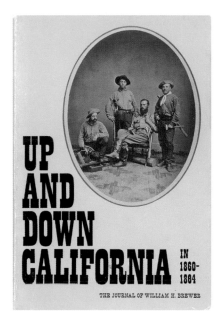

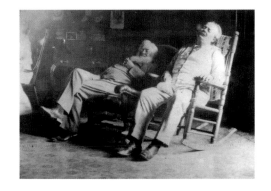

1857   1860   1861

Agoston Haraszthy, a Hungarian immigrant who titled himself "Count," settled in Sonoma and founded the Buena Vista winery there. A close friend of General Vallejo's, Haraszthy is often considered the father of the California wine industry for encouraging the planting of European grape varietals. In 1861, he sent back thousands of cuttings from a European vine-gathering tour. The following year he published a book on his winemaking experiences, outlining California's numerous virtues as a winemaking region. In the early days, when estate bottling was exceedingly rare, wine was commonly shipped in barrels—except for sparkling wine, as this photo of the Buena Vista winery by Eadweard Muybridge documents.

In an attempt to collect scientific data about its abundant resources after the frenzied years of the gold rush, the state of California commissioned William H. Brewer, a thirty-two-year-old Yale graduate, to complete a geological survey of the land within state lines. In 1860 Brewer and his party began in southern California and worked their way north, where in November 1861 they spent two weeks surveying Napa Valley. Brewer kept a journal of his impressions—including Napa's towns, farms, hot springs, and geysers—later published as *Up and Down California in 1860-1864*. About the hills east of the valley he wrote: "The lovely Napa Valley lies beneath us, with its pretty farms, its majestic trees, its vineyards and orchards and farmhouses." For the record, Brewer apparently drank cider—not wine—while in Napa Valley.

Charles Krug and Jacob Schram, both German immigrants, seem to have sipped their way into history. After working for Count Haraszthy in Sonoma, Krug moved over the mountains to Napa, where he served as winemaker to John Patchett, considered Napa's first commercial vintner. Krug went on to establish himself as Napa's preeminent vintner. A force majeure in the establishment of what would rapidly become Napa's most important industry, Krug founded his St. Helena winery in 1861—now the oldest in the Napa Valley. In 1862 Jacob Schram (above, left, with banker/vintner Charles Carpy) built Schramsberg, the valley's first hillside winery, hiring Chinese workers to dig the valley's first caves. At the height of the wine boom of the 1880s, Schram shipped vast quantities of wine each year to New York and Europe. *The Napa County Reporter,* founded in 1856, devoted much ink to the successful local industry.

1868

1869

1874

Sam Brannan, a squeaky wheel if ever there was one, spent years lobbying for a rail line to his Calistoga resort. He finally got his grease, so to speak. The Napa Valley Railroad arrived in 1868, and the following year was linked to the transcontinental railroad. The rails gave Napa winemakers a much-needed distribution alternative to shipping their product east around the treacherous horn. The railroad also brought an increasing ethnic and racial mix to the valley, especially in the town of Napa. St. Helena, for the most part, welcomed Germans attracted by the success of early pioneers such as Krug and Schram. Prior to the railroad, the stagecoach over the Lawley Toll Road was the only passage up valley after disembarking the San Francisco ferry at Suscol.

When the last spike was hammered into the last rail at Promontory, Utah, on May 10, 1869, the Union Pacific and Central Pacific Railroads linked America's two coasts. Displaced Chinese laborers—without whom Leland Stanford's transcontinental transport could not have been built—began flocking to the Napa Valley. They mined quicksilver, worked the vineyards, carved wine cellars out of limestone, and served as domestic help. Chinese laborers lived in the area now occupied by Meadowood, and grew rice in the dell where its golf course now exists. The network of stone walls and tunnels found throughout the area attests to the once-strong Chinese presence. During the 1880s, increasing anti-Chinese hostilities, including incidents of arson, forced many Chinese from the valley. Their departure made way for the influx of Italians who arrived during the next decade.

Every small town lives and dies in its local newspaper, and St. Helena is no different. The *St. Helena Star,* founded in 1874, proved to be a great supporter of the region's fledgling wine industry. Charles Gardner, who purchased the paper in 1876, regularly covered St. Helena's viticultural meetings—to the point, some said, where the up valley industry stole the thunder of Napa, the county seat. As historian William Heintz noted, "Every year, for almost 25 years, *The Star* published a column listing all Napa Valley wineries and the amount each produced in the fall crush. The column was widely reprinted in other news journals and brought a vast amount of publicity to Napa's wine industry." The *Star*'s stone headquarters, above, were erected in 1878.

82

1876

1878

1879

America's first great tidal wave of immigration occurred during the years between 1868 and 1888, when more than two million Germans crossed the Atlantic. Those Germans who came to the Napa Valley made profound contributions. Brothers Jacob, left, and Frederick Beringer, who founded Beringer Brothers Winery in 1876, hailed from Mainz, Germany. Jacob, who had been both a winemaker and a cooper in his native country, landed his first Napa job as winery foreman for Krug. In 1875 the Beringer brothers acquired 97 acres directly adjacent to Krug's for $14,500. Chinese laborers carved a limestone cellar, and by 1884 Frederick had started construction on the now historic Rhine House. The Beringer Brothers Winery remained open during Prohibition, distinguishing it as the valley's oldest continuously operating winery. It remained in the family until 1970.

Spa culture has long been integral to northern California, partly because of the area's geothermal assets, which make it—like Baden-Baden, and Bath—a natural resort, and partly because of the arrival in the 1870s of Seventh-Day Adventists, longtime advocates of healthy living. One prominent Adventist who settled in Napa Valley was Merritt G. Kellogg, brother of William Keith Kellogg, of cornflake fame. In 1878, he and two partners opened the Rural Health Retreat in St. Helena. This proto-spa, housed in a modest, two-story wood structure with a tent camp pitched next to a spring, beckoned to San Franciscans and offered "all the various forms of water vapors, hot air, medicated and electric baths, Swedish movements, proper exercise and rest." Kellogg's retreat has evolved into the St. Helena Hospital, the world's oldest continuously operating Seventh-Day Adventist hospital.

Gustave Niebaum, an enterprising Finn who like many new Americans changed the spelling of his name—in his case, from Nybom—founded the Inglenook Winery on land he had purchased around Rutherford and Oakville. He rapidly developed his venture into an oenophile's dream. The Inglenook Winery set a gold standard for Napa wines that wasn't bested until late in the twentieth century. Niebaum was both a scholar who was fluent in five languages and a student who pored over all of the period's available books on viticulture. He also visited Europe's leading wineries in an effort to learn the secrets of what was, for him, a grand passion and a mysterious and captivating art. Niebaum's efforts bore fruit: his wines became world renowned within a decade of Inglenook's inception and took gold and silver medals at the Paris Exposition of 1889.

1880

1881

1882

Soon after Scottish author Robert Louis Stevenson married Fanny Osbourne in San Francisco in 1880, the newlyweds headed north to honeymoon at Silverado, an abandoned mining town not far from Calistoga. There the couple remained until 1881. Two years later Stevenson published *The Silverado Squatters,* a memoir of his adventures in Napa Valley (excerpt, page 99). Stevenson penned the often quoted reference to Napa wine as "bottled poetry." He also equated the planting of vines to mining for gold, both—at least for him—a form of prospecting. Stevenson used many of his Silverado reflections about the untrammeled Napa landscape to create the wilderness world of *Treasure Island*. And he made sure to ship some of Napa's bottled poetry to Hawaii, the next treasured isle on the couple's grand tour.

By 1881, enough intrepid Italian Swiss souls had ventured west to establish an agricultural colony in Sonoma. They, too, entered the wine business, which at the time was in the midst of a boom so extraordinary that its like wouldn't occur for another century. The Italian Swiss cultivated European varietals to create wines that were soon bringing home medals from international competitions. By the early twentieth century, however, the flow of immigration to the U.S. had turned again: Italians, rather than Italian Swiss, began making the treacherous Atlantic crossing in droves. Many of them headed west, and later exerted considerable influence over the wine industry. The Italians also introduced olive oil, another homegrown and home-bottled product, to the Napa Valley.

In 1882 women's suffrage was not yet a national imperative, and women rarely worked outside the home. Necessity and tragic circumstances brought Hannah Weinberger, pictured above, into history as one of the Napa Valley's first recorded female vintners. Widowed by her husband's murder, Hannah Weinberger took over the winery founded by John C. Weinberger, one of the community's most respected vintners. Mrs. Weinberger won a silver medal at the Paris Exposition of 1889, the only woman among Napa's contingent of 11 award winners. Hannah had a friend and colleague in Josephine Tyson, also a widow, who made wine beginning in 1886.

1885

1889

1890

Tiburcio Parrott, president of the Sulphur Bank Mine during the quicksilver rush of the late-nineteenth century, objected strenuously to a clause of the 1879 California State Constitution that prohibited corporations holding state charters from employing "any Chinese or Mongolian." Once the constitution was adopted, work in the mines ceased because the Chinese provided the vast majority of subterranean labor. Parrott deliberately defied the law, and the circuit court ruled in his favor. Parrott was one of those California gentlemen who initiated the era of estate planting that swept through Napa—and elsewhere—as enormous wealth accumulated in America. The San Francisco–based financier built a mansion on Spring Mountain, planted his estate, and named it Miravalle. Within a decade, he was producing extremely sought-after wines, including California's most expensive cabernet.

William Bourn, a successful eastern merchant who headed west in 1850, made a fortune in mining and insurance. By 1869, he had gained control of the Empire Mine, which yielded nearly six million ounces of gold by its closing in 1957. After Bourn's death in 1874, his eldest son, twenty-two-year-old William Bourn II, took charge of the family empire, including a winery on sixty acres north of St. Helena. Junior commissioned Percy & Hamilton to design Greystone, a Richardsonian Romanesque pile of tufa stone completed in 1889. Launched as a semi-cooperative venture, it was California's largest wine facility, and its first with electricity. In 1894 Bourn sold the property to Christian Brothers, which held onto it for much of the twentieth century. It now houses the West Coast branch of the Culinary Institute of America.

Ambrose Bierce, iconoclastic author of *The Devil's Dictionary* and St. Helena resident (his home is now an inn), defined comfort as "a state of mind produced by the contemplation of a neighbor's uneasiness." Perhaps Len Owens, the San Francisco businessman who purchased the Aetna Springs Resort in 1890, found that to be true—but perhaps not. Owens commissioned Bernard Maybeck, the noted California architect, to design some of the buildings required to attract San Francisco's smart set; Owens also constructed a golf course on the property, reputed to be the first west of the Mississippi. The area around Aetna Springs was home to numerous quicksilver mines, discovered when Napa Valley's silver rush (silver was first discovered in King's Canyon, north of Calistoga, in the 1860s) failed to pan out. Cinnabar, as quicksilver (or mercury) was then called, was used to remove pure gold from ore.

85

1891

1893

1894

President Benjamin Harrison, like many politicians, campaigned on a whistle-stop tour. He later locomoted his way through the American West from April to May of 1891, traveling over 9,232 miles, the longest journey to date undertaken by any president while in office. Partly planned and largely financed by the former governor of California Leland Stanford, and scheduled so the president would be on hand for the dedication of Stanford University, Harrison's trip included a lavish banquet in the Garden Court of San Francisco's Palace Hotel, then the West Coast's finest hotel. The menu as planned had a great many French wines, but after considerable lobbying by local vintners, the list later included nine California wines as well as Eclipse, the "champagne" made by Count Haraszthy's son, Arpad.

By the early 1890s, phylloxera, a tiny aphid that destroys the rootstock of wine grapes, infested nearly half of Napa's vineyards. These insidious pests had plagued European vineyards a decade earlier, destroying most of the grape vines on the European continent. Phylloxera had already sneaked into the Napa Valley by the early 1880s. Krug, Niebaum, and Haraszthy had all brought vines from overseas, thereby colluding, however unwittingly, in the devastation. Phylloxera reduced what was a boom-year high of 16,000 to 18,000 Napa acres planted with grapes to 3,000 acres by 1900. Many farmers pulled out the vines and planted grain or fruit trees. Those who had the means to replant their vineyards did so with European varietals grafted onto resistant American rootstock—workers, like the woman above, sorted the roots for grafting.

Thanks to a transplanted Scot by the name of R. H. Pitchie, Napa was once known as the "County of Stone Bridges." Pitchie, a stonemason, constructed the stone bridges to replace the much more vulnerable wooden bridges. The Pope Street Bridge, above, was completed in 1894. The Putah Creek Bridge, once the largest stone bridge west of the Mississippi River, is now submerged under Lake Berryessa. (See facing page.)

1905   1906   1910

In 1905, the commute between Napa Valley and San Francisco took as little as two and a half hours: a 6:24 A.M. trolley left St. Helena, met the ferry at Vallejo, and deposited the traveler in San Francisco by 9 A.M. Trolley cars and automobiles conveyed more visitors than ever to Napa resorts and encouraged the weekend getaway, which started a building boomlet of weekend homes in what many considered an American Eden. Unlike the 1880s, however, few families moving to the Napa Valley were interested in winemaking. Real estate promotions for the area barely mentioned Napa wine production at the turn of the century. The advent of electricity, the telephone, the telegraph, as well as rapid public transportation, to say nothing of paved roads and the ever-more-affordable automobile, had begun to make the world seem a little smaller.

On the morning of April 18, 1906, the earth moved north of San Francisco. The city was virtually leveled by the devastating quake, and what didn't collapse was destroyed by fire. In addition to the loss of life and countless buildings reduced to rubble, the earthquake wreaked havoc on the wine industry, destroying two-thirds of the state's wine production. San Francisco's wine warehouses were hit hard, with the California Wine Association losing ten million gallons alone—the overall loss was estimated at forty-five million gallons. Many buildings in downtown Napa suffered damage, including the Revere House, above; many wineries were also severely damaged. It took several years for California's wine industry to replace the vast amount of wine that had been lost.

After the phylloxera years, the vineyards that had transformed the region during the boom time of the 1880s went the way of all flesh. In most cases, those farmers who survived the insect devastation replanted their still bountiful acres with prunes, cherries, pears, and walnuts. It took roughly half a century—until the 1960s and 1970s—for viticulture to make a serious comeback in the area. In addition to fruits and nuts, Napa Valley's agricultural enterprises also included numerous dairy farms. Napa County became one of the state's leading producers of prunes within the century's first decade, and by 1920 it had more acres in prunes than in grapes.

1913   1920   1933

Giving thanks is not solely an American tradition: the ritual predates Hermes' trip to the underworld to bring back Persephone, Demeter's straying daughter. Since the dawn of history, it has been a cultural imperative—for every culture—to set aside at least one day to honor the earth's produce. But America absolutely revels in its agricultural festivals. Gilroy, California, celebrates its garlic, for example; Palm Desert honors the date. In the late nineteenth century, St. Helena organized the Vintage Festival (pictured above in 1913), an annual autumn event with plays, pageants, and other festivities dedicated to the fruit of the vine. The festival continued attracting visitors into the mid-1930s. A decade ago St. Helena reinstituted its annual agricultural affair in a new guise: the Mustard Festival.

When the 18th Amendment passed into law on January 16, 1920, Americans literally found themselves announcing "last call." Temperance movements started around the country in the early nineteenth century. Later anti-alcohol crusaders upped the ante with a successful drive to abolish the sale of liquor coast to coast—including wine. Above, Michael and Louise Heitz, and their son Jack, share a last drink before closing the winery. The Feds did, however, permit the head of every household to make 200 gallons of "fruit juice" each year for home use, spurring a home-winemaking craze around the country. A writer for the *St. Helena Star* lamented, "The beautiful vineyards that have been the pride of the state are doomed." Sacramental wines remained legal, so a few Napa wineries, like Beaulieu and Christian Brothers, survived—even thrived—until Repeal.

When John Daniel Jr., Gustave Niebaum's grandnephew, took the helm of Inglenook in 1933, he ushered in the winery's golden age. Determined to maintain Inglenook's legacy of excellence, Daniel adhered to the almost supernaturally strict discipline that exceptionally high standards impose on winemaking, or any other pursuit. Daniel believed in "pride, not profit," according to his daughter Robin Lail. The wines that Daniel and his winemaker George Dueur produced from 1933 to 1964 were true to his motto. As the *Wine Spectator* noted, "Under Daniel, the grand Rutherford winery produced amazingly-long-lived Cabernets—wines that some still consider the best ever made in Napa."

1934   1935   1938

Repeal and the New Deal went hand in hand. In the depths of the Depression, liquor was once again legal. To educate a new generation in the hopes of reviving the moribund business, Beringer opened its doors to the public for guided tours and sales—the first winery to do so in Napa Valley. The period from 1934 to 1950 may have been even more difficult than the Prohibition years: wine production increased annually, grape prices fluctuated wildly, inflation sent the cost of equipment skyrocketing, yet the price of a fine bottle of wine held steady at less than a dollar. In 1939, the St. Helena Cooperative began to sell the grapes of dozens of Napa producers, helping to alleviate surpluses.

Wine and religion are as inseparable as sin and salvation. The complex relationship between the two is far older than the Miracle at Cana, and religious orders have long produced wines and spirits. The Christian Brothers, a Roman Catholic order, is a present-day American example of that notable tradition. The Christian Brothers began making wine in Martinez, California, in 1882, and moved to Napa's Mount Veeder in 1932. Brother Timothy Diener, above, was Christian Brothers' cellar master from 1935 until 1989. During his tenure Christian Brothers produced many award-winning wines and brandies. Diener served several times as president of the Napa Valley Vintners Association.

Andre Tchelistcheff was left for dead on a snow-covered battlefield in a blizzard during Russia's civil war, but he survived to discover wine and become one of California's legendary winemakers. When George de Latour of Beaulieu met Tchelitscheff, the Russian émigré was an agronomy student in France. De Latour invited him to move to California—the rest is history. Tchelistcheff is shown here with Madame Fernande de Latour, who ran Beaulieu after her husband died at age 84. Tchelistcheff's tenure at Beaulieu lasted for thirty-five years. Having established a wine lab in St. Helena, the man widely considered "the dean of American winemakers" shared his knowledge of winemaking with all comers. "Money is the dust of life," he said. "I don't have a wine cellar, I don't have a vineyard, I don't have nothing. I only have my head."

1941

1944

1949

Above is Carole Lombard at Beringer Brothers Winery, around the time she was starring in Alfred Hitchcock's *Mr. & Mrs. Smith*. America hadn't yet broken its isolationist stance, and the country was suffering shortages of luxury goods—imported wines, among other things. As the country's mood shifted, and as the war effort ramped up, California vineyards began to estate bottle their wines because of the diminishing number of tank cars available for shipping the product in bulk. Merchants on the East Coast, newly supportive of California wines, helped to develop a bigger market for domestic vintages. By the end of the war, the American palate had shifted to dry table wine and had turned homeward. As Frank Schoonmaker, the wine writer known as *le colonel,* noted in 1945, Americans no longer served California wine "with an apologetic smile or shrug."

In 1944, Louis Martini convinced a few friends and fellow vintners to meet regularly, and informally, to discuss the issues pertinent to their work and their industry—and the Napa Valley Vintners Association was born. It became a major force in the growth of the valley's wine industry. The founding officers are shown here, in 1959, a decade after they first met, posing with the actresses of *This Earth Is Mine*. The film, which starred Rock Hudson, Dorothy McGuire, Jean Simmons, Anna Lee, and Cindy Robbins, was shot in the Napa Valley. Martini (center) served as president, John Daniel Jr. (left) as vice president, and Robert Mondavi (right) as treasurer. Today, there are almost 250 members in the Vintners Association, which has met regularly at Meadowood, the site of the annual Napa Valley Wine Auction, for almost a quarter of a century.

After World War II, Americans took to the roads, and a web of mom-and-pop restaurants and drive-ins wove its way across America. For many, these roadside gems are the stuff that dreams—and love—are made of. Taylor's Refresher, which opened in 1949, was, and remains, just such a place in Napa Valley. As Adrienne Asher Gepford, an artist and writer who spent summer vacations in the Napa Valley of the 1950s, recalls: "There was nothing to compare to a double-dip chocolate cone at Taylor's." Until the mid-1960s, Taylor's was an *American Graffiti* kind of drive-in, with waitresses clipping trays of food to car windows. Taylor's menu, like Napa Valley, has changed over the years, but it is still a roadside stand, albeit one that serves ahi tuna burgers and white pistachio milk shakes. Taylor's has now taken its burgers on the road, opening an outpost in San Francisco's venerable Ferry Building.

1961

1964

1966

The connection between food and love runs deep, as Mary Frances Kennedy Fisher made so beautifully clear: "When I write of hunger, I am really writing about love and the hunger for it, and warmth and the love of it and it is all one." Fisher, one of the twentieth century's great writers on food and wine, spent the years from 1954 to 1970 traveling back and forth between France and St. Helena. In that time, she penned countless luminous essays as well as a shelfful of books, among them *How to Cook a Wolf, With Bold Knife and Fork, The Story of Wine in California* (excerpt, page 138), and *Consider the Oyster*. In 1961, she and fellow foodies Francis "Paco" Gould, Jim Beard, and a smorgasbord of supporters co-founded the Napa Valley Wine Library.

Freeman Nicholls, Meadowood's founder, had interesting connections. Mildred Smith Nicholls, his wife, was the daughter of Francis Marion "Borax" Smith (1846-1931), who once owned the Claremont Hotel in Berkeley, California, and made a fortune in the "Twenty Mule Team" Borax Mining Company, an icon of the American West. But Nicholls was a visionary in his own right. A lumber magnate and developer, he first envisioned Meadowood as Madrone Knoll, upscale homes anchored by club-style dining and recreational facilities. Jamie and Jack Davies, a couple who had recently moved to the old Jacob Schram property, were among Meadowood's first members. "I played tennis there," said Mrs. Davies. "It was a family-oriented place." Nonie Travers of Mayacamas Vineyards also recalled the estate's early days, "It was a low-key, local kind of place, as the valley was in those days."

When Robert Mondavi convinced his parents, Cesare and Rosa Mondavi, to buy the Charles Krug Winery in 1943 for $75,000, he launched a family dynasty that was instrumental in the valley's growth into a world-renowned center of food and wine. In 1966, he founded his namesake winery, the first major winery to open in the valley since Prohibition. (The story of his departure from Krug, the family winery that he and his brother Peter ran, is the stuff of legend.) Mondavi has long been acknowledged as the Napa Valley's greatest ambassador. With Margrit Biever Mondavi, whom he married in 1980, Mondavi bolstered respect for Napa wines abroad, partly by instituting the winery's "Great Chefs" program.

1968   1971   1975

During the Age of Aquarius, the air of America was filled with "isms." Valley dwellers were trying to determine the valley's future, and in the process they necessarily parsed the merits of activism, self-determinism, environmentalism, progressivism, conservatism, and, indeed, agriculturalism. Faced with a rapidly growing population, and after a very contentious process, the Napa County Board of Supervisors in 1968 adopted a landmark environmental ordinance, the Agricultural Preservation Act (or Ag Preserve), designed to protect the valley's agricultural character. The Ag Preserve limited the use and development of zoned areas, ordering that land could not be subdivided into parcels smaller than twenty acres. The original stipulations of the Ag Preserve have been modified over the years, and the size of the parcels increased to 160 acres, but the spirit of the legislation still reigns.

An advertising jingle once advised Americans to "look for the union label"— and many did. In the late 1960s, the United Farm Workers, under the leadership of Cesar Chavez, had organized successful boycotts of lettuce and grapes. As Chavez and the union gained a toehold in Napa, the growers, in direct response, created the Growers Foundation in 1971. Higher wages and better work conditions ensued. At the time, migrant Mexican workers came to the valley in revolving crews: they first pruned the vines, then, later in the season, another crew picked the grapes. That changed over the next two decades. Thanks to increased hand harvesting, more intense canopy management, and near constant planting of new vineyards, what was once temporary labor has evolved into year-round employment, a sea change that impelled a major growth spurt in the Napa Valley's Mexican community.

Biology may be destiny, but in the wine industry, in the 1970s, it was all about chemistry, at least for Lisa Van de Water. Van de Water, a chemist, established the Wine Lab, an independent testing service, in 1975—just as the women's movement hit its stride. One of the first prominent females in what was then a resolutely male industry, Van de Water raised awareness about the role that fermentation and microbiology play in winemaking: "It didn't matter if I had purple hair if I could tell them what was wrong with their wine." Margrit Biever, who later married Robert Mondavi, encountered a much more skeptical audience when, a decade earlier, she was the first female tour guide at the Krug Winery: "I can't tell you how many times I heard, 'What does a woman know about wine?'"

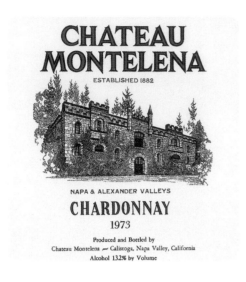

1976

1977

1978

Throughout its brief history, America has offered many surprises to the French—from Ben Franklin to Lindbergh to liberation. At the now legendary Paris Tasting of 1976, part of America's bicentennial celebrations, we arrivistes on the world scene pulled off another stunning cultural coup d'état. The event was a blind tasting by a noted panel of French wine specialists—a modern Judgment of Paris conceived and produced by Steven Spurrier, an English wine merchant and educator. As Spurrier recalled, "The French panel was determined not to put a California wine on top, but when they did, the news traveled around the world." Warren Winiarski's '73 Stag's Leap Cabernet received the golden apple for the reds, while the '73 Chateau Montelena Chardonnay led among the white wines. All but three of the California wines came from the Napa Valley, a fact that put Napa and its wines back on the map.

In the early 1970s, Alice Waters opened her legendary Berkeley restaurant, Chez Panisse, serving only the freshest products, locally grown and in season—a revolutionary concept that formed the basis for California cuisine. In 1977, Domaine Chandon opened the first restaurant housed in a Napa winery, a pairing that underscored the happily symbiotic relationship between food and wine, or, in this case, great wine and haute cuisine. A year later, Philippe Jeanty (above, far left) became the restaurant's executive chef at the tender age of twenty-one. His high standards, and those of his colleagues, helped to spark an entirely new industry—that of the small specialty farm—as well as a flowering of great restaurants in Napa Valley.

By the late 1970s, the Napa Valley was on the verge of an industry boom. Aside from Zelma Long, who had succeeded Mike Grgich as oenologist at the Robert Mondavi Winery in 1972, few women had made their mark in the cellar. But the times were changing. Cathy Corison was among the first women to benefit from the boom: she became the winemaker at Yverdon, a small winery on Spring Mountain. "The wine business was exploding in Napa, and there just weren't enough experienced winemakers around, giving me and so many others a great opportunity," Corison remembered. Two years later, she moved to the Chappellet winery. She wasn't alone: during the next two decades, women like Helen Turley, Heidi Barrett, and Mia Klein established themselves as members of a very select group, Napa Valley's most sought-after winemakers.

1979

1981

1983

The year that H. William Harlan, Peter Stocker, and John Montgomery acquired Meadowood was the year that Mother Teresa received the Nobel Peace Prize and a first class stamp cost fifteen cents. Meadowood's transformation from modest country club to luxury resort was celebrated in June with a three-day opening gala with a formal dinner and a display of Napa's agricultural bounty. Molly Chappellet (shown above with her family) commissioned artist Dorau Gazet to create inflatable sculpture, to enliven the Meadowood landscape. Shortly thereafter, Meadowood became the headquarters of the Napa Valley Vintners Association and the home of the annual Napa Valley Wine Auction. In 1987, it became one of the state's first members of Relais & Chateaux.

Why is the first time always the hardest? In the case of the initial Napa Valley Wine Auction, it was the heat. In fact, that's the first thing that everyone remembers about that June day. The temperature soared under the tents at Meadowood, sending the corks popping on some of the silent auction wines and bursting the balloons fashioned as grape clusters—a key element of Molly Chappellet's décor. "The wine auction was an opportunity to allow vintners to create a funding base that didn't previously exist for Napa charities, and to bring the quality of Napa's vineyards and wineries to the public's attention," says Jamie Davies, who volunteered on that day, as did so many others. The event succeeded spectacularly on both counts, so much so that it has become an annual event. To date, the auction has generated more than $50 million for local hospitals and community organizations.

The American dream is alive and well in Napa Valley. Just ask the Ceja family, among the first members of the Mexican-American community to become vineyard owners and winemakers. After years in the bracero work program, Pablo Ceja, the family patriarch, immigrated to Napa Valley in 1967. In 1983, the full family pooled its resources to buy land in the Carneros region. The third generation of the family (above, left to right, Pedro Ceja, Amelia Moran Ceja, Martha Ceja, and Armando Ceja), all of whom are children of immigrant farm workers, now joins the company principals in running the Ceja Vineyard, which the family established in 1999. Amelia Moran Ceja, company president, has been instrumental in the winery's rapid rise to prominence, and Armando Ceja, winemaker, is crafting notable Ceja wines.

THE FRENCH LAUNDRY COOKBOOK
THOMAS KELLER

1987   1994   2000

Association croquet is not for the faint of heart. Like chess, the point of croquet is to vanquish your opponent. There are strategies for this, such as the "Chernobyl Opening," which is exactly what it sounds like: blasting your opponent out of the game before he has an opportunity to hit the ball. This test of strategy and touch is as polite on the surface as the game's perfectly manicured playing fields, and all the more devastating for it. Meadowood hosted the Pro-American Croquet Tournament in 1987—the first in the world with prize money. Above are Cindy Pawlcyn and Robert Mondavi with Jerry Stark (far right), Meadowood's resident professional, a top-ranked player in the U.S. Pawlcyn, Meadowood's founding chef who went on to establish Mustards, one of Napa Valley's finest restaurants, is grinning because she trounced Wolfgang Puck in tournament play.

America cherishes the true original. That, at least, has been Thomas Keller's experience with the French Laundry, the restaurant he re-launched in Yountville in 1994 (the original opened in 1978, in a building that once housed a French steam laundry). Keller's goal? To create a three-star destination. Soon enough, he had. Food critics straightaway began singing the praises of Keller's innovative cuisine. Ruth Reichl, reviewing it for *The New York Times,* called the French Laundry "the most exciting place to eat in the United States." It's also among the most difficult, with reservations available only months in advance. Keller has gone on record about Napa Valley as a mecca for the restaurant renaissance that occurred in the 1980s and 1990s: "It's the only place in the country where people come specifically to drink excellent wines and eat fine food."

The new millennium dawned on the twentieth annual Napa Valley Wine Auction, and with it the rational exuberance that had contributed over the years to making the annual June sale the world's most important wine auction—and Napa's most prominent charitable and social event. The proceeds in 2000 were carbonated, like the Nasdaq and the Dow: the auction raised $9.5 million, with an average of $47,195 per live lot. The record lots that year included $700,000 for a ten-vintage vertical of magnums from Harlan Estate, and $500,000, a single-bottle record, for an Imperial of Screaming Eagle Cabernet Sauvignon. By 2004 the auction had raised a total of more than $50 million in its twenty-four years, all of which benefited two local hospitals, as well as youth and farmworkers' housing programs.

98

2001

2003

2004

In the forty years that make up Napa Valley's recent renaissance, life in America has changed profoundly. Food and wine—lore and legend, innovation and experiment have become cultural currency. The West Coast branch of the Culinary Institute of America, opened in 1995, affirms Napa Valley's unique role in today's culinary culture. Based in the historic Greystone Winery, the C.I.A.'s Napa Valley center for continuing education offers courses for food and wine professionals. As early as 1988, Robert and Margrit Mondavi, along with the Julia Child, and other leaders in the wine community, began to explore the idea of establishing a unique cross-disciplinary institution devoted to food and wine. In 2001, the American Center for Food, Wine, and the Arts—COPIA—opened its doors. Partly an educational institute and partly a research facility, COPIA is both an original and a first, like much else in Napa Valley.

Meadowood celebrates its fortieth anniversary. The property carries on its role as a traditional part of the family, social, cultural, and viticultural values that are essential to the Napa Valley way of life. It also serves as a home away from home for visitors who enjoy the serenity and hospitality of the wine country. Founded as a private club in 1964, Meadowood became an early gathering place for the valley's burgeoning wine community and the home of the Napa Valley Wine Auction. Over the next twenty-five years the property progressed along with Napa Valley itself. Today, Meadowood continues its integral role in the evolution of Napa Valley life and carries on as a center of the valley's wine community.

The Napa Valley Reserve, a private 80 acre winegrowing estate flowing from the foothills of Howell Mountain to the Napa River, accepts its first members. This parcel of land has a history reflective of Napa Valley as a whole. It first supported the Wappo Indians, then the Spanish Empire, which later ceded it via the Mexican Land Grants to General Mariano Vallejo. John Howell purchased it when California joined the union; he and his descendants ranched and farmed it for fifty years. The Marolfs, Swiss immigrants, acquired it at the turn of the twentieth century, and farmed it for the next 100 years. In 2001, The Napa Valley Reserve was formed for discerning wine lovers to experience the next level of winegrowing.

THE SILVERADO
SQUATTERS

Napa Valley has been long a seat of the winegrowing industry. It did not here begin, as it does too often, in the low valley lands along the river, but took at once to the rough foot-hills, where alone it can expect to prosper. A basking inclination, and stones, to be a reservoir of the day's heat, seem necessary to the soil for the wine; the grossness of the earth must be evaporated, its marrow daily melted and refined for ages; until at length these clods that break below our footing, and to the eye appear but common earth, are truly and to the perceiving mind, a masterpiece of nature. The dust of Richebourg, which the wind carries away, what an apotheosis of the dust! Not man himself can seem a stranger child of that brown, friable powder, than the blood and sun in that old flask behind the faggots.

A Californian vineyard, one of man's outposts in the wilderness, has features of its own. There is nothing here to remind you of the Rhine or Rhone, of the low *Côte d'Or,* or the infamous and scabby deserts of Champagne; but all is green, solitary, covert. We visited two of them, Mr. Schram's and Mr. M'Eckron's, sharing the same glen.

Some way down the valley below Calistoga, we turned sharply to the south and plunged into the thick of the wood. A rude trail rapidly mounting; a little stream tinkling by on the one hand, big enough perhaps after the rains, but already yielding up its life; overhead and on all sides a bower of green and tangled thicket, still fragrant and still flower-bespangled by the early season, where thimble-berry played the part of our English hawthorn, and the buck-eyes were putting forth their twisted horns of blossom: through all this, we struggled toughly upwards, canted to and fro by the roughness of the trail, and continually switched across the face by sprays of leaf or blossom. The last is no great inconvenience at home; but here in California it is a matter of some moment. For in all woods and by every wayside there prospers an abominable shrub or weed, called poison-oak, whose very neighbourhood is venomous to some, and whose actual touch is avoided by the most impervious.

The two houses, with their two vineyards, stood each in a green niche of its own in this steep and narrow forest dell. Though they were so near, there was already a good difference in level; and Mr. M'Eckron's head must be a long way under the feet of Mr. Schram. No more had been cleared than was necessary for cultivation; close around each oasis ran the tangled wood; the glen enfolds them; there they lie basking in sun and silence, concealed from all but the clouds and the mountain birds.

Mr. M'Eckron's is a bachelor establishment; a little bit of a wooden house, a small cellar hard by in the hillside, and a patch of vines planted and tended single-handed by himself. He had but recently began; his vines were young, his business young also; but I thought he had the look of the man who succeeds. He hailed from Greenock: he remembered his father putting him inside Mons Meg, and that touched me home; and we exchanged a word or two of Scotch, which pleased me more than you would fancy.

Mr. Schram's, on the other hand, is the oldest vineyard in the valley, eighteen years old, I think; yet he began a penniless barber, and even after he had broken ground up here with his black malvoisies, continued for long to tramp the valley with his razor. Now, his place is the picture of prosperity: stuffed birds on the verandah, cellars far dug into the hillside, and resting on pillars like a bandit's cave: —all trimness, varnish, flowers, and sunshine, among the tangled wildwood. Stout, smiling Mrs. Schram, who has been to Europe and apparently all about the States for pleasure, entertained Fanny in the verandah, while I was tasting wines in the cellar. To Mr. Schram this was a solemn office; his serious gusto warmed my heart; prosperity had not yet wholly banished a certain neophite and girlish trepidation, and he followed every sip and read my face with proud anxiety. I tasted all. I tasted every variety and shade of Schramberger, red and white Schramberger, Burgundy Schramberger, Schramberger Hock, Schramberger Golden Chasselas, the latter with a notable bouquet, and I fear to think how many more. Much of it goes to London—most, I think; and Mr. Schram has a great notion of English taste.

In this wild spot, I did not feel the sacredness of ancient cultivation. It was still raw, it was no Marathon, and no Johannisberg; yet the stirring sunlight, and the growing vines, and the vats and bottles in the cavern, made a pleasant music for the mind. Here, also, earth's cream was being skimmed and garnered; and the London customers can taste, such as it is, the tang of the earth in this green valley. So local, so quintessential is a wine, that it seems the very birds in the verandah might communicate a flavour, and that romantic cellar influence the bottle next to be uncorked in Pimlico, and the smile of jolly Mr. Schram might mantle in the glass.

But these are but experiments. All things in this new land are moving farther on: the wine-vats and the miner's blasting tools but picket for a night, like Bedouin pavillions; and to-morrow, to fresh woods! This stir of change and these perpetual echoes of the moving footfall, haunt the land. Men move eternally, still chasing Fortune; and, Fortune found, still wander. As we drove back to Calistoga, the road lay empty of mere passengers, but its green side was dotted with the camps of travelling families: one cumbered with a great waggonful of household stuff, settlers going to occupy a ranche they had taken up in Mendocino, or perhaps Tehama County; another, a party in dust coats, men and women, whom we found camped in a grove on the roadside, all on pleasure bent, with a Chinaman to cook for them, and who waved their hands to us as we drove by.

—Robert Louis Stevenson

excerpt from *The Silverado Squatters,* 1883

4

Life in the Vineyard

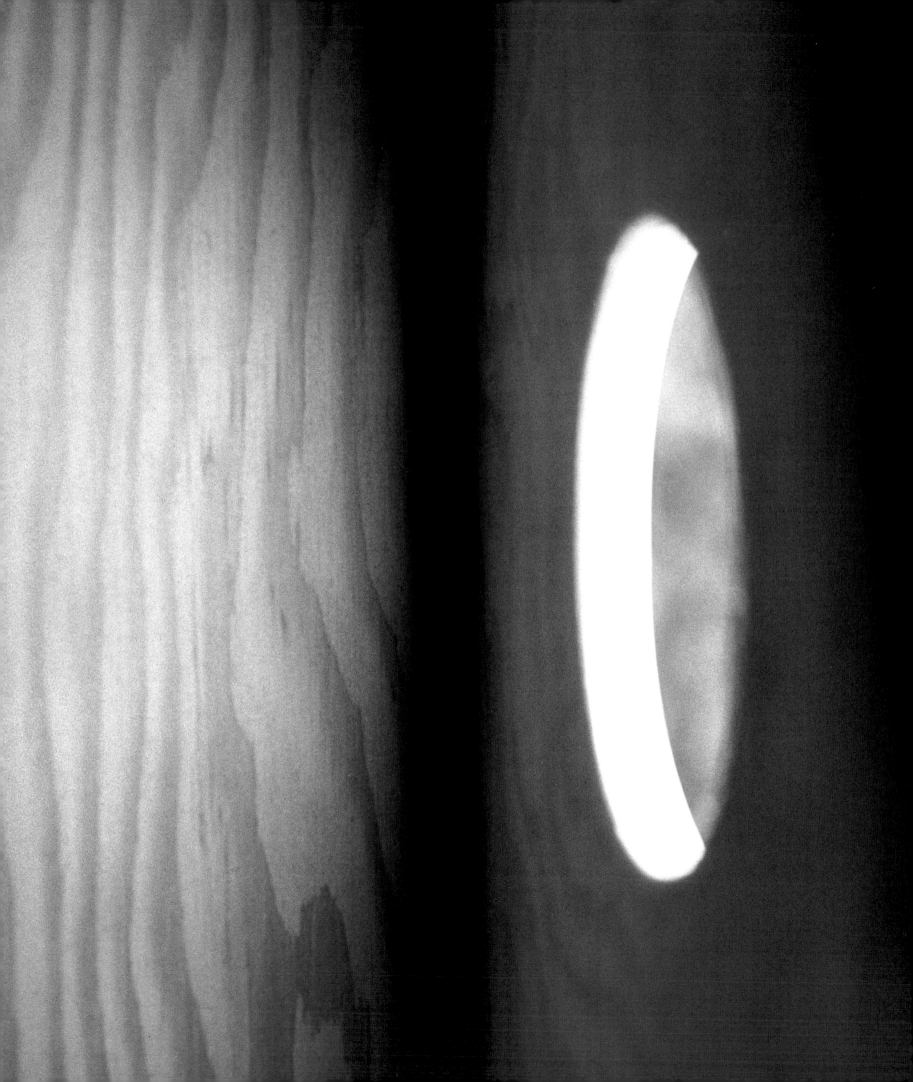

VINEYARD
TRANSFORMATIONS

When I held the first cluster of grapes harvested from the vineyard that my husband and I planted in 1973, I wanted to save it forever—as a symbol of achievement. Two years of building calluses on my hands and feet as I planted, cultivated, and pruned my young vines had resulted in a small but credible crop of premium wine grapes. That first, fist-sized bunch of Pinot Noir was tangible proof that European wine grapes could indeed thrive in a place where skeptics had said they couldn't. So instead of sending that cluster to the fermenting vat with the rest of the fruit, I put it in a clear glass jar, covered it with formaldehyde, and set it on the windowsill of my wine lab.

Twenty-six years later, having sold the vineyard, I decided to get rid of that jar of puckered fruit, too. How naïve I had been to think that pickling a cluster of grapes could stop time at that moment of glory, the harvest. But as I drove away from the vineyard for the final time, I dried my tears and began to reflect on what my years as a vintner had meant. I realized, slowly, that in growing grapes and transforming them into wine, I, too, had been transformed.

Each step of the process had changed me. I was seven months pregnant with my first child as I bent down and dug a hole for each of thousands of grape vines. It was springtime, and new life was everywhere. Birds were building nests in the hedgerow as I repeated the motions of digging, planting, digging, planting, all while feeling the activity of the child within me. Planting grapes carried the same element of hope and trust as pregnancy. I told myself that all would be well, and worth the labor.

The young vines flourished, and my daughter was born. I wore her on my back as she and the vines taught me their next lesson: there is no such thing as putting off the demands and needs of either child or plant. I could no longer sleep the morning away, read in the afternoon, or expect that I could take a bath and stay clean for more than a few hours. My friends wondered—some of them loudly— why I wanted to work so hard, and why I couldn't get someone else to hoe the vines.

They missed the point. It was in the physical acts—of pulling weeds, of tying the lengthening vines to stakes, of nursing and bathing my child—that my attachment grew. There was no room or time for resentment. The tactile sensations of grooming the vine were like touching my baby's skin. This was what I wanted to do, and where I wanted to be.

When drought came to the vineyard that first summer, we raced around trying to get water to the struggling vines. A neighboring farmer helped us resurrect an old irrigation pump, and we watched the wilted leaves straighten up and turn their faces to the sun. Had this old neighbor not been willing to neglect his own farm while he helped us save ours, we would never have harvested anything. Having begun our grape-growing venture with the arrogance of youth and the assumption that we could figure it all out ourselves, my husband and I were humbled by the generosity of our neighbor.

Winter came, and the green leaves turned yellow, then brown. The vineyard became a tangle of dead-looking wood. That was an illusion. How astonishing it was to prune those vines and see brilliant green inside every brown cane. When spring returned, I could almost watch the buds swelling until they burst forth with tiny, pink-tipped green leaves. As the first leaves unfurled, they revealed the primordial clusters that would bloom several weeks later, perfuming the night sky as each berry was pollinated.

Each season brought with it a piece of a larger pattern. After bloom came *veraison,* when the berries turned color and began to ripen. At harvest, there was another great transformation as we picked the fruit, de-stemmed and crushed it. A froth of yeast reproducing in a frenzy converted the sugar in the grapes to alcohol. And wine was born. Young wines are like the young vines that have produced them: full of promise, but not all that they will become. Again, there is a leap of faith, and the hope that everything will turn out well.

As one season led to another, as I gave birth again and watched my children grow among the vines, I began to see that wanting something will not make it so. Working from dawn to dusk will not prevent the depredations of insects and storms, nor, in the case of children, earaches and tantrums. Nothing is certain. And with winemaking, there is only one chance each year to choose the best moment to harvest, to orchestrate the fermentation.

I learned to be ready to act at a moment's notice and at the same time to exercise patience. The seasons impose a rhythm to life, while each day presents the unpredictable. No matter how much my mind's eye could foresee the coming day, including problems that I knew I would have to solve, the true challenges always came out of left field, completely unforeseen.

Fortunately, every spring offers renewal. As the vineyard flourishes, so too does the wine silently evolving down in the cellar. The sad pickled cluster of grapes that I had saved from my first harvest was a poor symbol of what we had really achieved. That can be glimpsed, if just barely, in the fleeting experience of tasting the wines that my husband and I made, together, over the years. The heady exaltation that I feel as I inhale the intricate aromas that took their time developing reminds me that as my newly planted vines grew and bore fruit, and as that fruit was transformed into wine, so my family and I were transformed by a richness of experience that blends both joy and sadness into love.

— Louisa Thomas Hargrave

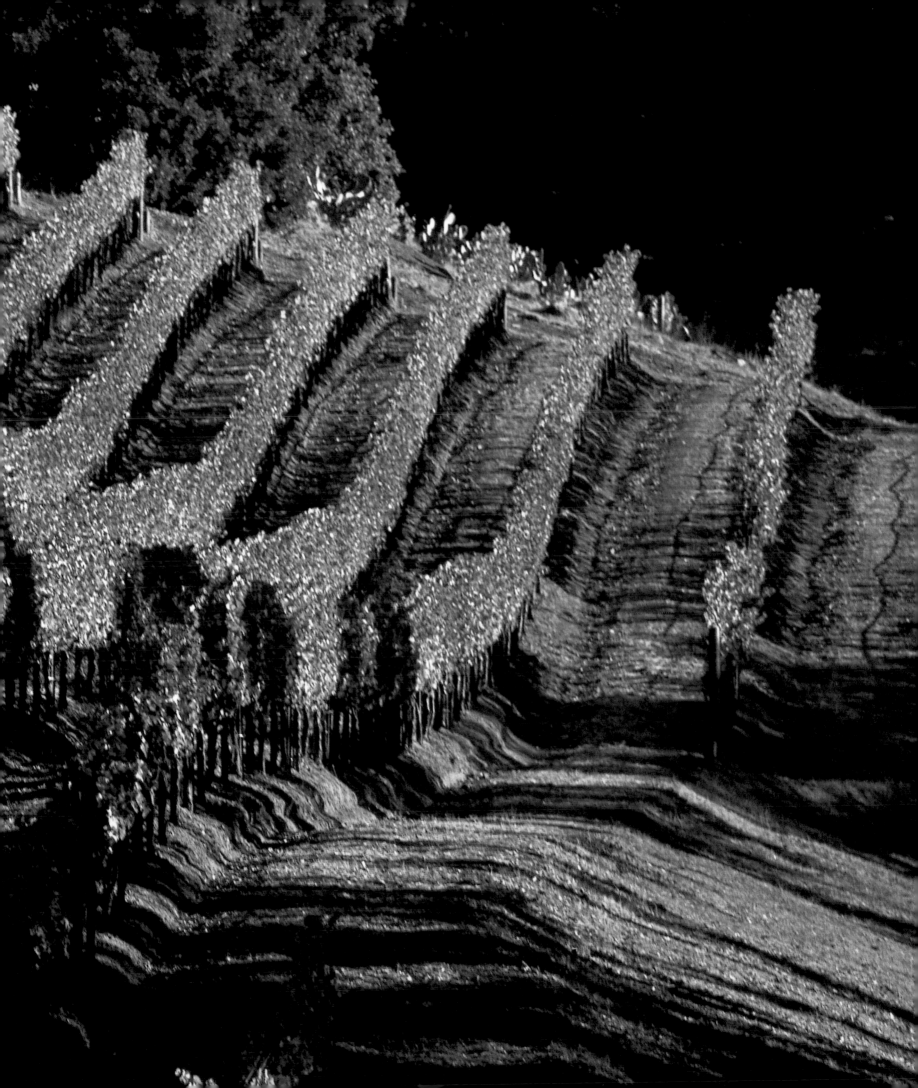

VINEYARD WORKER

I live in Napa, in a mobile home in Grandview near the Marquez Ranch. I have been there six years, and working in Napa for twenty. I learned to work the vineyards here. I learned, basically, by coming here and just planting the grapes, tending to the vines, pruning the plants, and harvesting them. Through that, one learns how to care for the plants. Slowly one learns, little by little. For years I worked with a crew that had more experience than I did, so every year I learned more and more. Then I learned to drive the tractor, the sprayer, the cultivator. The plants are different each year, and my job is different each day. It depends on the time, on the weather, and I like that. I know that my work, and the work of my community, is very important to the Napa Valley.

I miss my wife's cooking—she makes really good Oaxaca mole. On weekends, I visit my brother, who has his family here, and I do home chores—wash clothes, buy groceries. Every once in a while, on the weekend, I'll go out to a restaurant for Mexican food or Chinese food. I cook, and my sister-in-law makes pretty good food, but not as good as my wife. The immigration papers are being processed to bring my wife and three children to the U.S., and maybe in about two years they will come. I think I will work here at least until my daughters finish school—about another five years or so—and then go back.

The end of the season is best because I get to go to Mexico. When I get off the bus in Oaxaca my family is there—my kids, wife, and

mother. Later my sisters come to visit. When I am home I am always together with my wife. I work on my home, and I am reconstructing my house a little more every year. When I meet someone in Mexico they can kind of tell that I work in America by my clothes and the way I dress. People in Oaxaca see the difference—that one lives better than the people that live in the town there. Working here is a very big sacrifice because you want the best for your kids, and it is very hard to be away from them—I talk to my family over the phone each week.

My family and I are very involved in our community and our church in Oaxaca. Every church has a saint's day, especially in the wintertime. Our church's saint is the Virgin of Jukila. I help with the festivities for January 8th. If you visited Oaxaca, I would take you on a little trip to the Tule Tree, a big tree, and also to the ruins of Mitla, the churches and stores, and the market on Sundays.

—Elfego Martinez

BOB STEINHAUER'S TERRAIN

One Halloween when I was in high school, a bunch of kids were at my house, and my father said, "You guys are going to go out and get in trouble, right?" Of course we said, "No." My dad laughed. And one of the kids said, "Mr. Steinhauer, what did you do when you were our age?" He said, "We would go around and turn over all the outhouses." So we went outside thinking that was a pretty good idea, but that there were no outhouses around. Then we realized there was a trucking company right down the street that had an outhouse, and we decided to turn it over. We did, but there happened to be a big trucker inside, and he chased us—if he'd caught us, he would have killed us. When we got home, my dad asked what we had done, and we told him about the outhouse and the mad trucker. My dad said, "You damn fools, you ought to know that you always turn an outhouse over on its door!" My dad was a good thinker, and in his way he was trying to tell us to think through problems.

My dad worked for Safeway Stores for thirty-seven years, and when I was very young—I was born in Exeter, California, in 1941—he managed a Safeway in the San Joaquin Valley. When I was eleven, my parents bought my grandfather's raisin vineyard outside of Fresno, and we moved to the heart of California's raisin-growing district. My grandfather had bought the property around 1920. It was about twenty acres, which is really small, so my dad had to work another job just to support the family. I started in the vineyards when I was fourteen, doing tractor work and irrigation work and other tasks. All my uncles were raisin farmers, and I worked for them in the summers; my mother's family also had a raisin vineyard, so there was always a lot of work to do.

When I had time I would ride around on the fender of my uncle Roy's tractor, and he taught me a lot about farming and encouraged me to be a viticulturist. He was in the sixth wave at Omaha Beach, and he had a big influence on my life.

When I graduated from high school in 1959, I decided that raisin growing on that scale was too hard. I was motivated to go to college, and I worked my way through school in a grocery store and got my bachelor's degree in viticulture. I studied under a remarkable and renowned viticulturist named Vince Petrucci—another person who helped shape my life. I had to take genetics, biology, plant physiology, and all the regular courses. I lived at home then, and I'd get back late from work and my mom would always have a sandwich for me and sit down and talk to me. We did a lot of things as a family, and that was a great help to me.

I started my career in table grapes. I worked for a company that was owned by Richard Bagdasarian, a fascinating man who taught me a lot in a short period of time. I ended up managing a crew of Philippino workers, then I had a crew of Yemeni men who packed table grapes. Working with people who had come to the United States from the

Philippines and from Yemen was really interesting. They were a great bunch of people, and I started to learn a lot more about the world.

In 1965, a company called Schenley Industries hired me. They made Roma Wines and Cornet Brandy. They had a five-thousand-acre vineyard in the Delano area, and I was assistant manager. I had people reporting to me who had been managing that property for more years than I had been alive. I quickly learned a lot about trying to manage people, and in about 1967, after two years there, I decided to return to Fresno State to get my master's degree. I was in the first class at Fresno State to receive a master's in plant science—it required courses in statistics, soils and irrigation, chemistry, biology, you name it.

My wife, Verna Grimm, and I went to high school together, but we lost track of each other after graduation. In 1968, though, I was living in Fresno and so was Verna; we got married later that year. She was a teacher, and she helped me get my master's degree by teaching school. When I graduated, Schenley offered me a position in Delano—paying more than we ever thought I'd ever make, $12,000 a year, so we went back to Delano. Verna got a job teaching school there, and we were very happy. I got to know Cesar Chavez and Dolores Huerta, and negotiated a couple of contracts with the United Farm Workers.

We came up to Napa in 1971, when I was hired by Andy Beckstoffer, who is a major landowner in Napa Valley and another person who greatly influenced my life. At that time, he worked for Heublein, which had just purchased Beaulieu. I reported to Andre Tchelistcheff—a real stroke of luck for me, because at the time I didn't know anything about farming in Napa Valley, and Andre was setting the standard for California wines. He has influenced so many contemporary winemakers. Andre trained in France, and it was he who really taught me about the importance of soils and where the best grapes could be grown, given the climate and the soils and the habitat of each site. Andre and I eventually became really close. He would always have us over for Orthodox Easter—we were always worried about frost at that time of year, so Verna and I couldn't leave to go see our families in Fresno—and we'd have him for our Easter.

About that same time, I was lucky enough to be one of thirty people accepted into the first Agriculture Leadership Program, which was initially funded by the Kellogg Foundation, among others, and which included training in communications, political science, economics, and the arts. The program's purpose was to broaden you and make you a leader in the industry, and that's exactly what it did. I was from a small town, and hadn't been outside California. We went to the opera and the theater in London and Los Angeles, we toured Watts after the riots, we went all over the U.S., Mexico, and Europe. I got to see Richard Chamberlain in *Richard II* at the Kennedy Center; that was a hell of an event in my life. Those experiences broadened my perspective about the world, and about agriculture in general; the program also helped me to understand the value of being involved in industry policy issues.

In 1978, a guy named Bob Bakota called me and asked if I would be interested in working for Beringer. Beringer had a wine master named

Myron Nightingale, who had worked for Schenley. I knew him, and he was doing great things. So, in 1979, after really thinking it over, I took the job. Since then, the company has grown fairly dramatically. I think we had a couple thousand acres, primarily in the Napa Valley, when I first came to work here twenty-five years ago. I've grown up with Beringer. Last July, they named a vineyard after me: Steinhauer Ranch. At one point they asked me what my favorite vineyard was, and I said this particular vineyard, a beautiful vineyard in Angwin. It was a total surprise to me. I absolutely cried. They've put a big gate in now, with little plaques on each side that say, "Steinhauer Ranch."

I'm currently president of the Napa Valley Vintners Association. I'm on the board of the California Wine Institute, involved with the Napa Valley Wine Growers, and I'm also on a statewide board that is working to combat a new pest in California, the glassy-winged sharp-shooter.

Right now the Napa Valley Vintners Association has two major goals. One is to promote the Napa Valley, which is what it has done from the beginning. The other is to raise money for the community through the wine auction: we have put $50 million back into the community to date. Our other efforts involve public policy. We're coming out with a Green Certification Program, among other environmental initiatives: we spend a great deal of effort trying to make this valley an even better place to live.

One of my goals as president is to make sure that as many members as possible are actively involved, so that we can get the message out to the community that we are good stewards and good citizens. For me, being part of the Napa Valley Vintners Association is a way of paying back both the community and the vintners who have made this such a great place.

I think the wines in Napa Valley continue to improve. I remember another one of my mentors, Joe Heitz, of Heitz Cellars, years ago told me, "You know, we need to quit trying to emulate the French. We need to make Napa Valley wines." Well, once we made that adjustment, we stopped being children of the French. We grew up, and we became adults making our own style of wines. The people who own wineries and are making wines are so eclectic and so diverse in their backgrounds, and such great artists, that I see nothing but a very positive future for the Napa Valley.

I have a bit of intuitiveness about where to plant things and how to grow things, and I think I've contributed to the valley in a small way, but I've certainly gotten a lot more out of the industry than I could ever possibly give back. If they put "He was a good farmer" on my tombstone, I'll be very happy with that.

—Bob Steinhauer

His memory was an album full of images
of grapes and leaves and twigs in color.

Idwal Jones, *The Vineyard*

5

The Aesthetics of Wine

THE STORY OF WINE
IN CALIFORNIA

Four hundred years before the birth of Christ, a Greek named Theognis wrote, "Wine is wont to show the mind of man."

More than two thousand years later, in 1920, a wise old Englishman named George Saintsbury wrote about wines in his *Notes on a Cellar Book:* "When they were good they pleased my senses, cheered my spirits, improved my moral and intellectual powers, besides enabling me to confer the same benefits on other people."

Both men, so far apart in time but akin in their broad understanding of their fellows as well as of themselves, agreed with poets and philosophers of every civilization since the first real one that good wine, well drunk, can lend majesty to the human spirit.

How to drink it, once it is poured from its flask or bottle, depends mainly upon the man who does it. It can be a sottish thing, rank with gluttony and brutality, and then its punishment is as sure as hell itself, and as sure an indication of the fool within.

If wine be well drunk, it is as Theognis and Saintsbury said, an indication of a man's spirit as well as of his general attitude toward the rest of his world.

Once in the glass, there are a few simple things which will bring out its character for anyone who looks for more than a liquid to run down his gullet and inspire his soul.

The rules are simple, and if followed will add pleasure to the simplest palate, the simplest meal, and make it grow.

First, each wine should have its own glass, or be rinsed between wines. The glass, preferably stemmed, should be filled only one-third or one-half full.

The rest of it is a natural progression toward the swallowing and then the instinctive wait for the aftertaste, that strange sensory enjoyment which must follow even a sip of decent wine, and which can be like a touch of paradise after a great one.

First, then, the glass should be held against the light of sky or candles or of fire on the hearth, if one is with good friends, or against any light at all—a picnic on a hill, a waterside restaurant, a railroad station between trains.

It will hold in it what Robert Louis Stevenson once called the "blood and the sun in that old flask," and sometimes it will cling tantalizingly to the sides, shifting the light with it, and sometimes it will be as aloof as crystal itself, seeming to disdain what it is held in.

The next step is to savor. What is called the bouquet is the reward for this enjoyable operation, and it can vary from the delicate to the robust. If the wine is cold, the bouquet will be a longer and often more subtle discovery than at room temperature of the smell itself, and the glass can be rotated gently to make the unmistakable odor of this wine or that rise and fume invisibly into the nostrils of its seeker.

Some of the great wines are as much their own bouquet as taste or color or aftertaste, and there are special glasses almost like fat-bottomed chimney pots for the benefit of their sniffers. But for most persons, as well as for most wines, the plainest of glasses—from a tumbler to a simple stemmed glass which will hold any white as well as any red wine—will give ample pleasure to us.

The next step—and by no means the most important, although it is the basic reason for this whole agreeable rigmarole—is to drink the wine.

Sips of it are the best. A great draught is for thirst, and should be left to water, man's ally. A small sip is enough, to begin the full enjoyment of any wine at all. It should be rolled under the tongue and then over it, no matter how unobtrusively, to make all the taste buds spring to their full attention. It can be held for a few seconds in the mouth. Then it rolls down the throat like a blissful messenger of what's to follow, and the promise is good: what is eaten will taste better, and what follows the eating and the drinking will be worthy of them.

There is much written these days about the "ceremonies" of wine tasting and wine drinking, and there is, perhaps of necessity, much balderdash and plain as well as fancy snobbery in it. Perhaps one of the most sensible comments on this pompous attempt to make people take the natural function of wine drinking in snob fashion has been said by the owner of a French chateau, one of the greatest of the Bordeaux wineries: "...Wine is a pleasure, not a puzzling and dreadful duty."

Another good writer about wine enjoyment has said lately in one of the excellent house organs put out by California vintners and growers, "Learn to analyze your sensations and record them in your memory. By so doing, you will recognize the same or similar wine when you meet it again."

This is a most rewarding feeling to any conscious thinking man, whether he wants a bottle of reputable "Red Ink" with his steak or a bottle of champagne to celebrate his daughter's wedding: he knows what he is looking for and what he can spend for it and how much it will give to him. He knows what will please *him,* and will enable him, as Saintsbury said, "to confer the same benefits on other people."

He may have no desire, as do some serious as well as flamboyant "connoisseurs," to be able to recognize a certain year of a certain bottling of a certain section of a certain vineyard, but he will know what he wants: a good red or white or rosé wine from one of California's winegrowing districts, and even, with some practice, the same wine from this or that valley—Santa Clara, San Bernardino, Livermore, Sonoma, Napa. It will be one more door opened to his appreciation of the rare things of life.

He will be able to agree with Shakespeare that "Good wine is a good familiar creature if it be well used."

—M. F. K. Fisher, excerpt from
The Story of Wine in California, 1962

WINE AND THE
APPRECIATION OF LIFE

Heraclitus told us you can never step into the same river twice "for other waters are ever flowing on to you." Likewise, you can never drink the same wine twice. The appreciation of wine, for all that we may try to quantify it, is, in the end, a subjective experience. Not only does fine wine continue to grow and develop in the bottle and in the glass, to change from one day to the next in response to barometric pressure and other variables, but our appreciation of any given wine from the same maker and vintage, even from the same barrel, is subject to our own quirks of receptivity, to the place and the company in which we drink it, to the knowledge we bring with us, and the food with which we pair it. In order to develop an appreciation of wine, it's true, we agree to the objective fiction; we attempt to isolate it from contextual variables, to treat the glass in front of us as if it contains a stable and quantifiable substance. But ultimately, the love of wine should lead us back to an appreciation of a larger realm of the senses—to the social context and the natural world in which it is produced and enjoyed.

We Americans still have a lot to learn about wine. Not in the technical sense. The California winery industry, led by Robert Mondavi and a few other early visionaries in the Napa Valley, has pioneered some of the technical breakthroughs which have resulted in cleaner, richer, fresher tasting wines around the world. Likewise American

wine critics, led by Robert Parker, have democratized and revitalized what used to be an arcane and clubby branch of knowledge, and stolen the lead from the British. Considering that not long ago the phrase *California wine* belonged more or less in the same book of oxymorons as, say, *Dutch cuisine,* this is saying a lot.

The next step for American wine lovers is to broaden their vision and relax: to see wine as just another aspect of the well-lived life. In Europe, where wine has been a part of daily life for thousands of years, American oenophiles are sometimes viewed as monomaniacs— zealous and somewhat narrow-minded converts to a generous and pantheistic faith. But give us a little time—it's been less than forty years since Mondavi opened his eponymous winery in Oakville, and less than thirty since a flight of Napa Valley wines defeated some of the top growths of France at the famous "Judgment of Paris" tasting organized by Steven Spurrier. As for Meadowood, it was a sleepy property in 1966, the same year that Mondavi opened his winery; the seven rooms available at the time enjoyed little more than a 30 percent occupancy rate and the idea of wine tourists flocking to the Napa Valley seemed quixotic.

The more I learn about wine, the more wine teaches me about the world around me. My interest in the grape has led me to some of the more beautiful parts of the world—Alsace, Tuscany, Provence, the Cape of Good Hope, the Willamette Valley, to name a few—and brought me into contact with some of the most stimulating and con- genial eccentrics of our time. Wine people are as a rule gregarious, generous, and passionate. The cult of Bacchus doesn't include many anal-retentive personalities. I learned a lot about viticulture from Angelo Gaja over dinner at a trattoria in Barberesco, but what I remember most vividly was the story of how he smashed his television set with a sledgehammer after he decided his kids were watching too much. And I'll never forget Joan Dillon at Chateau Haut-Brion talking about hijinks on President Kennedy's yacht, or Allen Ginsberg disrobing in the offices of *The Paris Review*. Our love of wine is the fraternal bond that brings us together, and it is the lubricant that stimulates our conversation, but it's a polygamous relationship which encourages and enhances our other passions. It leads us to other subjects and leads us back to the world.

I discovered the wines of Napa Valley many years ago, and eventually the wine led me to the place itself. I encountered there not only a unique landscape and climate but a community of rugged individualists, an extraordinary and at times improbable mix of talent, ambition, and idealism. The Napa Valley is a microcosm. And it is also, though it took us a little while to realize it, a *terroir*—that is, a unique concatenation of soil, climates, and topography—or, rather, dozens of *terroirs*. You don't *have* to visit Napa, walk the vineyards, and meet the people who make the wine in order to enjoy it, but doing so inevitably enhances the experience you bring to the wine and the pleasure you take from it, as more and more oenophiles have discovered.

Although in many ways Napa's preeminence is recent, its winemaking tradition goes back a hundred and fifty years; the first commercial wine was produced in 1857. A few years later German immigrant Charles Krug had moved to the valley and begun to make wine; another German immigrant, Jacob Beringer, worked as Krug's foreman for eight years before starting his own winery just down the road. By the 1880s Napa wines were attracting national and even international attention. In many ways it seems to have been created for winegrowing, its climate and soils among the most perfect in the world for that purpose. After a visit to the valley in 1880, Robert Louis Stevenson wrote, "Here earth's cream was being skimmed and garnered" to produce what he called "bottled poetry."

Like poetry, the appreciation of wine challenges our intellectual faculties, our senses, and our emotions. It summons memories and enriches our understanding of the natural world. It lifts us up and delivers us from the mundane circumstances of daily life, inspires contemplation, and ultimately it returns us to that very world, refreshed, with enriched understanding and appreciation.

—Jay McInerney

TASTE

There were six of us to dinner that night at Mike Schofield's house in London: Mike and his wife and daughter, my wife and I, and a man called Richard Pratt. Richard Pratt was a famous gourmet. He was president of a small society known as the Epicures, and each month he circulated privately to its members a pamphlet on food and wines. He organized dinners where sumptuous dishes and rare wines were served. He refused to smoke for fear of harming his palate, and when discussing a wine, he had a curious, rather droll habit of referring to it as though it were a living being. "A prudent wine," he would say, "rather diffident and

evasive, but quite prudent." Or, "a good-humored wine, benevolent and cheerful—slightly obscene, perhaps, but nonetheless good-humored."

I had been to dinner at Mike's twice before when Richard Pratt was there, and on each occasion Mike and his wife had gone out of their way to produce a special meal for the famous gourmet. And this one, clearly, was to be no exception. The moment we entered the dining room, I could see that the table was laid for a feast. The tall candles, the yellow roses, the quantity of shining silver, the three wineglasses to each person, and above all, the faint scent of roasting meat from the kitchen brought the first warm oozings of saliva to my mouth.

As we sat down, I remembered that on both Richard Pratt's previous visits Mike had played a little betting game with him over the claret, challenging him to name its breed and its vintage. Pratt had replied that that should not be too difficult provided it was one of the great years. Mike had then bet him a case of the wine in question that he could not do it. Pratt had accepted, and had won both times. Tonight I felt sure that the little game would be played over again, for Mike was quite willing to lose the bet in order to prove that his wine was good enough to be recognized, and Pratt, for his part, seemed to take a grave, restrained pleasure in displaying his knowledge.

The meal began with a plate of whitebait, fried very crisp in butter, and to go with it there was a Moselle. Mike got up and poured the wine himself, and when he sat down again, I could see that he was watching Richard Pratt. He had set the bottle in front of me so that I could read the label.

It said, "Geierslay Ohligsberg, 1945." He leaned over and whispered to me that Geierslay was a tiny village in the Moselle, almost unknown outside Germany. He said that this wine we were drinking was something unusual, that the output of the vineyard was so small that it was almost impossible for a stranger to get any of it. He had visited Geierslay personally the previous summer in order to obtain the few dozen bottles that they had finally allowed him to have.

"I doubt anyone else in the country has any of it at the moment," he said. I saw him glance again at Richard Pratt. "Great thing about Moselle," he continued, raising his voice, "it's the perfect wine to serve before a claret. A lot of people serve a Rhine wine instead, but that's because they don't know any better. A Rhine wine will kill a delicate claret, you know that? It's barbaric to serve a Rhine before a claret. But a Moselle—ah!—a Moselle is exactly right."

Mike Schofield was an amiable, middle-aged man. But he was a stock-broker. To be precise, he was a jobber in the stock market, and like a number of his kind, he seemed to be somewhat embarrassed, almost ashamed to find that he had made so much money with so slight a talent. In his heart he knew that he was not really much more than a bookmaker—an unctuous, infinitely respectable, secretly unscrupulous bookmaker—and he knew that his friends knew it, too. So he was seeking now to become a man of culture, to cultivate a literary and aesthetic taste, to collect paintings, music, books, and all the rest of it. His little sermon about Rhine wine and Moselle was a part of this thing, this culture that he sought.

"A charming little wine, don't you think?" he said. He was still watching Richard Pratt. I could see him give a rapid furtive glance down the table

each time he dropped his head to take a mouthful of whitebait. I could almost feel him waiting for the moment when Pratt would take his first sip, and look up from his glass with a smile of pleasure, of astonishment, perhaps even of wonder, and then there would be a discussion and Mike would tell him about the village of Geierslay.

But Richard Pratt did not taste his wine. He was completely engrossed in conversation with Mike's eighteen-year-old daughter, Louise. He was half turned toward her, smiling at her, telling her, so far as I could gather, some story about a chef in a Paris restaurant. As he spoke, he leaned closer and closer to her, seeming in his eagerness almost to impinge upon her, and the poor girl leaned as far as she could away from him, nodding politely, rather desperately, and looking not at his face but at the topmost button of his dinner jacket.

We finished our fish, and the maid came around removing the plates. When she came to Pratt, she saw that he had not yet touched his food, so she hesitated, and Pratt noticed her. He waved her away, broke off his conversation, and quickly began to eat, popping the little crisp brown fish quickly into his mouth with rapid jabbing movements of his fork. Then, when he had finished, he reached for his glass, and in two short swallows he tipped the wine down his throat and turned immediately to resume his conversation with Louise Schofield.

Mike saw it all. I was conscious of him sitting there, very still, containing himself, looking at his guest. His round jovial face seemed to loosen slightly and to sag, but he contained himself and was still and said nothing.

Soon the maid came forward with the second course. This was a large roast of beef. She placed it on the table in front of Mike who stood up and carved it, cutting the slices very thin, laying them gently on the plates for the maid to take around. When he had served everyone, including himself, he put down the carving knife and leaned forward with both hands on the edge of the table.

"Now," he said, speaking to all of us but looking at Richard Pratt. "Now for the claret. I must go and fetch the claret, if you'll excuse me."

"You go and fetch it, Mike?" I said. "Where is it?"

"In my study, with the cork out—breathing."

"Why the study?"

"Acquiring room temperature, of course. It's been there twenty-four hours."

"But why the study?"

"It's the best place in the house. Richard helped me choose it last time he was here."

At the sound of his name, Pratt looked around.

"That's right, isn't it?" Mike said.

"Yes," Pratt answered, nodding gravely. "That's right."

"On top of the green filing cabinet in my study," Mike said. "That's the place we chose. A good draft-free spot in a room with an even temperature. Excuse me now, will you, while I fetch it."

The thought of another wine to play with had restored his humor, and he hurried out the door, to return a minute later more slowly, walking softly, holding in both hands a wine basket in which a dark bottle lay. The label was out of sight, facing downward. "Now!" he cried as he came toward the table. "What about this one, Richard? You'll never name this one!"

Richard Pratt turned slowly and looked up at Mike; then his eyes travelled down to the bottle nestling in its small wicker basket, and he raised his eyebrows, a slight, supercilious arching of the brows, and with it a pushing outward of the wet lower lip, suddenly imperious and ugly.

"You'll never get it," Mike said. "Not in a hundred years."

"A claret?" Richard Pratt asked, condescending.

"Of course."

"I assume, then, that it's from one of the smaller vineyards?"

"Maybe it is, Richard. And then again, maybe it isn't."

"But it's a good year? One of the great years?"

"Yes, I guarantee that."

"Then it shouldn't be too difficult," Richard Pratt said, drawling his words, looking exceedingly bored. Except that, to me, there was something evil, and in his bearing an intentness that gave me a faint sense of uneasiness as I watched him.

"This one is really rather difficult," Mike said, "I won't force you to bet on this one."

"Indeed. And why not?" Again the slow arching of the brows, the cool, intent look.

"Because it's difficult."

"That's not very complimentary to me, you know."

"My dear man," Mike said, "I'll bet you with pleasure, if that's what you wish."

"It shouldn't be too hard to name it."

"You mean you want to bet?"

"I'm perfectly willing to bet," Richard Pratt said.

"All right, then, we'll have the usual. A case of the wine itself."

"You don't think I'll be able to name it, do you?"

"As a matter of fact, and with all due respect, I don't," Mike said. He was making some effort to remain polite, but Pratt was not bothering overmuch to conceal his contempt for the whole proceeding. And yet, curiously, his next question seemed to betray a certain interest.

"You like to increase the bet?"

"No, Richard. A case is plenty."

"Would you like to bet fifty cases?"

"That would be silly."

Mike stood very still behind his chair at the head of the table, carefully holding the bottle in its ridiculous wicker basket. There was a trace of whiteness around his nostrils now, and his mouth was shut very tight.

Pratt was lolling back in his chair, looking up at him, the eyebrows raised, the eyes half closed, a little smile touching the corners of his lips. And again I saw, or thought I saw, something distinctly disturbing about the man's face, that shadow of intentness between the eyes, and in the eyes themselves, right in their centers where it was black, a small slow spark of shrewdness, hiding.

"So you don't want to increase the bet?"

"As far as I'm concerned, old man, I don't give a damn," Mike said. "I'll bet you anything you like."

The three women and I sat quietly, watching the two men. Mike's wife was becoming annoyed; her mouth had gone sour and I felt that at any moment she was going to interrupt. Our roast beef lay before us on our plates, slowly steaming.

"So you'll bet me anything I like?"

"That's what I told you. I'll bet you anything you damn well please, if you want to make an issue out of it."

"Even ten thousand pounds?"

"Certainly I will, if that's the way you want it." Mike was more confident now. He knew quite well that he could call any sum Pratt cared to mention.

"So you say I can name the bet?" Pratt asked again.

"That's what I said."

There was a pause while Pratt looked slowly around the table, first at me, then at the three women, each in turn. He appeared to be reminding us that we were witness to the offer.

"Mike!" Mrs. Schofield said. "Mike, why don't we stop this nonsense and eat our food. It's getting cold."

"But it isn't nonsense," Pratt told her evenly. "We're making a little bet."

I noticed the maid standing in the background holding a dish of vegetables, wondering whether to come forward with them or not.

"All right, then," Pratt said. "I'll tell you what I want you to bet."

"Come on, then," Mike said, rather reckless. "I don't give a damn what it is—you're on."

Pratt nodded, and again the little smile moved the corners of his lips, and then, quite slowly, looking at Mike all the time, he said, "I want you to bet me the hand of your daughter in marriage."

Louise Schofield gave a jump. "Hey!" she cried. "No! That's not funny! Look here, Daddy, that's not funny at all."

"No, dear," her mother said. "They're only joking."

"I'm not joking," Richard Pratt said.

"It's ridiculous," Mike said. He was off balance again now.

"You said you'd bet anything I liked."

"I meant money."

"You didn't *say* money."

"That's what I meant."

"Then it's a pity you didn't say it. But anyway, if you wish to go back on your offer, that's quite all right with me."

159

"It's not a question of going back on my offer, old man. It's a no-bet anyway, because you can't match the stake. You yourself don't happen to have a daughter to put up against mine in case you lose. And if you had, I wouldn't want to marry her."

"I'm glad of that, dear," his wife said.

"I'll put up anything you like," Pratt announced. "My house, for example. How about my house?"

"Which one?" Mike asked, joking now.

"The country one."

"Why not the other one as well?"

"All right then, if you wish it. Both my houses."

At that point I saw Mike pause. He took a step forward and placed the bottle in its basket gently down on the table. He moved the saltcellar to one side, then the pepper, and then he picked up his knife, studied the blade thoughtfully for a moment, and put it down again. His daughter, too, had seen him pause.

"Now, Daddy!" she cried. "Don't be *absurd!* It's *too* silly for words. I refuse to be betted on like this."

"Quite right, dear," her mother said. "Stop this at once, Mike, and sit down and eat your food."

Mike ignored her. He looked over at his daughter and he smiled, a slow, fatherly, protective smile. But in his eyes, suddenly, there glimmered a little triumph. "You know," he said, smiling as he spoke. "You know, Louise, we ought to think about this a bit."

"Now, stop it, Daddy! I refuse even to listen to you! Why, I've never heard anything so ridiculous in my life!"

"No, seriously, my dear. Just wait a moment and hear what I have to say."

"But I don't *want* to hear it."

"Louise! Please! It's like this. Richard, here, has offered us a serious bet. He is the one who wants to make it, not me. And if he loses, he will have to hand over a considerable amount of property. Now, wait a minute, my dear, don't interrupt. The point is this. *He cannot possibly win.*"

"He seems to think he can."

"Now listen to me, because I know what I'm talking about. The expert, when tasting a claret—so long as it is not one of the famous great wines like Lafite or Latour—can only get a certain way toward naming the vineyard. He can, of course, tell you the Bordeaux district from which the wine comes, whether it is from St. Emilion, Pomerol, Graves, or Médoc. But then each district has several communes, little counties, and each county has many, many small vineyards. It is impossible for a man to differentiate between them all by taste and smell alone. I don't mind telling you that this one I've got here is a wine from a small vineyard that is surrounded by many other small vineyards, and he'll never get it. It's impossible."

"You can't be sure of that," his daughter said.

"I'm telling you I can. Though I say it myself, I understand quite a bit about this wine business, you know. And anyway, heavens alive, girl, I'm your father and you don't think I'd let you in for—for something you didn't want, do you? I'm trying to make you some money."

"Mike!" his wife said sharply. "Stop it now, Mike, please!"

Again he ignored her. "If you will take this bet," he said to his daughter, "in ten minutes you will be the owner of two large houses."

"But I don't want two large houses, Daddy."

"Then sell them. Sell them back to him on the spot. I'll arrange all that for you. And then, just think of it, my dear, you'll be rich! You'll be independent for the rest of your life!"

"Oh, Daddy, I don't like it. I think it's silly."

"So do I," the mother said. She jerked her head briskly up and down as she spoke, like a hen. "You ought to be ashamed of yourself, Michael, ever suggesting such a thing! Your own daughter, too!"

Mike didn't even look at her. "Take it!" he said eagerly, staring hard at the girl. "Take it quick! I'll guarantee you won't lose."

"But I don't like it, Daddy."

"Come on, girl. Take it!"

Mike was pushing her hard. He was leaning toward her, fixing her with two hard bright eyes, and it was not easy for the daughter to resist him.

"But what if I lose?"

"I keep telling you, you can't lose. I'll guarantee it."

"Oh, Daddy, must I?"

"I'm making you a fortune. So come on now. What do you say, Louise? All right?"

For the last time, she hesitated. Then she gave a helpless little shrug of the shoulders and said, "Oh, all right, then. Just so long as you swear there's no danger of me losing."

"Good!" Mike cried. "That's fine! Then it's a bet!"

"Yes," Richard Pratt said, looking at the girl. "It's a bet."

Immediately, Mike picked up the wine, tipped the first thimbleful into his own glass, then skipped excitedly around the table filling up the others. Now everyone was watching Richard Pratt, watching his face as he reached slowly for his glass with his right hand and lifted it to his nose. The man was about fifty years old and he did not have a pleasant face. Somehow, it was all mouth—mouth and lips—the full, wet lips of the professional gourmet, the lower lip hanging

downward in the center, a pendulous, permanently open taster's lip, shaped open to receive the rim of a glass or a morsel of food. Like a keyhole, I thought, watching it; his mouth is like a large wet keyhole.

Slowly he lifted the glass to his nose. The point of the nose entered the glass and moved over the surface of the wine, delicately sniffing. He swirled the wine gently around in the glass to receive the bouquet. His concentration was intense. He had closed his eyes, and now the whole top half of his body, the head and neck and chest, seemed to become a kind of huge sensitive smelling-machine, receiving, filtering, analyzing the message from the sniffing nose.

Mike, I noticed, was lounging in his chair, apparently unconcerned, but he was watching every move. Mrs. Schofield, the wife, sat prim and upright at the other end of the table, looking straight ahead, her face tight with disapproval. The daughter, Louise, had shifted her chair away a little, and sidewise, facing the gourmet, and she, like her father, was watching closely.

For at least a minute, the smelling process continued; then, without opening his eyes or moving his head, Pratt lowered the glass to his mouth and tipped in almost half the contents. He paused, his mouth full of wine, getting the first taste; then he permitted some of it to trickle down his throat and I saw his Adam's apple move as it passed by. But most of it he retained in his mouth. And now, without swallowing again, he drew in through his lips a thin breath of air which mingled with the fumes of the wine in the mouth and passed on down into his lungs. He held the breath, blew it out through his nose, and finally began to roll the wine around under the tongue, and chewed it, actually chewed it with his teeth as though it were bread.

It was a solemn, impressive performance, and I must say he did it well.

"Um," he said, putting down the glass, running a pink tongue over his lips. "Um—yes. A very interesting little wine—gentle and gracious, almost feminine in the aftertaste."

There was an excess of saliva in his mouth, and as he spoke he spat an occasional bright speck of it onto the table.

"Now we can start to eliminate," he said. "You will pardon me for doing this carefully, but there is much at stake. Normally I would perhaps take a bit of a chance, leaping forward quickly and landing right in the middle of the vineyard of my choice. But this time—I must move cautiously this time, must I not?" He looked up at Mike and he smiled, a thick-lipped, wet-lipped smile. Mike did not smile back.

"First, then, which district in Bordeaux does this wine come from? That is not too difficult to guess. It is far too light in the body to be from either St. Emilion or Graves. It is obviously a Médoc. There's no doubt about *that*.

"Now—from which commune in Médoc does it come? That also, by elimination, should not be too difficult to decide. Margaux? No. It cannot be Margaux. It has not the violent bouquet of a Margaux. Pauillac? It cannot be Pauillac, either. It is too tender, too gentle and wistful for a Pauillac. The wine of Pauillac has a character that is almost imperious in its taste. And also, to me, a Pauillac contains just a little pith, a curious, dusty, pithy flavor that the grape acquires from the soil of the district. No, no. This—this is a very gentle wine, demure and bashful in the first taste, emerging shyly but quite graciously in the second. A little

arch, perhaps, in the second taste, and a little naughty also, teasing the tongue with a trace, just a trace, of tannin. Then, in the aftertaste, delightful—consoling and feminine, with a certain blithely generous quality that one associates only with the wines of the commune of St. Julien. Unmistakably this is a St. Julien."

He leaned back in his chair, held his hands up level with his chest, and placed the fingertips carefully together. He was becoming ridiculously pompous, but I thought that some of it was deliberate, simply to mock his host. I found myself waiting rather tensely for him to go on. The girl Louise was lighting a cigarette. Pratt heard the match strike and he turned on her, flaring suddenly with real anger. "Please!" he said. "Please don't do that! It's a disgusting habit, to smoke at table!"

She looked up at him, still holding the burning match in one hand, the big slow eyes settling on his face, resting there a moment, moving away again, slow and contemptuous. She bent her head and blew out the match, but continued to hold the unlighted cigarette in her fingers.

"I'm sorry, my dear," Pratt said, "but I simply cannot have smoking at table."

She didn't look at him again.

"Now, let me see—where were we?" he said. "Ah, yes. This wine is from Bordeaux, from the commune of St. Julien, in the district of Médoc. So far, so good. But now we come to the more difficult part—the name of the vineyard itself. For in St. Julien there are many vineyards, and as our host so rightly remarked earlier on, there is often not much difference between the wine of one and the wine of another. But we shall see."

He paused again, closing his eyes. "I am trying to establish the 'growth,'" he said. "If I can do that, it will be half the battle. Now, let me see. This wine is obviously not from a first-growth vineyard—nor even a second. It is not a great wine. The quality, the—the—what do you call it?—the radiance, the power, is lacking. But a third growth—that it could be. And yet I doubt it. We know it is a good year—our host has said so—and this is probably flattering it a little bit. I must be careful. I must be very careful here."

He picked up his glass and took another small sip.

"Yes," he said, sucking his lips, "I was right. It is a fourth growth. Now I am sure of it. A fourth growth from a very good year—from a great year, in fact. And that's what made it taste for a moment like a third—or even a second-growth wine. Good! That's better! Now we are closing in! What are the fourth-growth vineyards in the commune of St. Julien?"

Again he paused, took up his glass, and held the rim against that sagging, pendulous lower lip of his. Then I saw the tongue shoot out, pink and narrow, the tip of it dipping into the wine, withdrawing swiftly again—a repulsive sight. When he lowered the glass, his eyes remained closed, the face concentrated, only the lips moving, sliding over each other like two pieces of wet, spongy rubber.

"There it is again!" he cried. "Tannin in the middle taste, and the quick astringent squeeze upon the tongue. Yes, yes, of course! Now I have it! This wine comes from one of those small vineyards around Beychevelle. I remember now. The Beychevelle district, and the river and the little harbor that has silted up so the wine ships can no longer use it. Beychevelle...could it actually be a Beychevelle itself? No, I don't think so. Not quite. But it is somewhere very

close. Château Talbot? Could it be Talbot? Yes, it could. Wait one moment."

He sipped the wine again, and out of the side of my eye I noticed Mike Schofield and how he was leaning farther and farther forward over the table, his mouth slightly open, his small eyes fixed upon Richard Pratt.

"No. I was wrong. It was not a Talbot. A Talbot comes forward to you just a little quicker than this one; the fruit is nearer to the surface. If it is a '34, which I believe it is, then it couldn't be Talbot. Well, well. Let me think. It is not a Beychevelle and it is not a Talbot, and yet—yet it is so close to both of them, so close, that the vineyard must be almost in between. Now, which could that be?"

He hesitated, and we waited, watching his face. Everyone, even Mike's wife, was watching him now. I heard the maid put down the dish of vegetables on the sideboard behind me, gently, so as not to disturb the silence.

"Ah!" he cried. "I have it! Yes, I think I have it!"

For the last time, he sipped the wine. Then, still holding the glass up near his mouth, he turned to Mike and he smiled, a slow, silky smile, and he said, "You know what this is? This is the little Château Branaire-Ducru."

Mike sat tight, not moving.

"And the year, 1934."

We all looked at Mike, waiting for him to turn the bottle around in its basket and show the label.

"Is that your final answer?" Mike said.

"Yes, I think so."

"Well, is it or isn't it?"

"Yes, it is."

"What was the name again?"

"Château Branaire-Ducru. Pretty little vineyard. Lovely old château. Know it quite well. Can't think why I didn't recognize it at once."

"Come on, Daddy," the girl said. "Turn it round and let's have a peek. I want my two houses."

"Just a minute," Mike said. "Wait just a minute." He was sitting very quiet, bewildered-looking, and his face was becoming puffy and pale, as though all the force was draining slowly out of him.

"Michael!" his wife called sharply from the other end of the table. "What's the matter?"

"Keep out of this, Margaret, will you please."

Richard Pratt was looking at Mike, smiling with his mouth, his eyes small and bright. Mike was not looking at anyone.

"Daddy!" the daughter cried, agonized. "But, Daddy, you don't mean to say he's guessed it right!"

"Now, stop worrying my dear," Mike said. "There's nothing to worry about."

I think it was more to get away from his family than anything else that Mike then turned to Richard Pratt and said, "I'll tell you what, Richard. I think you and I better slip off into the next room and have a little chat?"

"I don't want a little chat," Pratt said. "All I want is to see the label on that bottle." He knew he was a winner now; he had the bearing, the quiet arrogance of a winner, and I could see that he was prepared to become thoroughly nasty if there was any trouble. "What are you waiting for?" he said to Mike. "Go on and turn it round."

Then this happened: The maid, the tiny, erect figure of the maid in her white-and-black uniform, was standing beside Richard Pratt, holding something out in her hand. "I believe these are yours, sir," she said.

Pratt glanced around, saw the pair of thin horn-rimmed spectacles that she held out to him, and for a moment he hesitated. "Are they? Perhaps they are. I don't know."

"Yes sir, they're yours." The maid was an elderly woman—nearer seventy than sixty—a faithful family retainer of many years standing. She put the spectacles down on the table beside him.

Without thanking her, Pratt took them up and slipped them into his top pocket, behind the white handkerchief.

But the maid didn't go away. She remained standing beside and slightly behind Richard Pratt, and there was something so unusual in her manner and in the way she stood there, small, motionless, and erect, that I for one found myself watching her with a sudden apprehension. Her old gray face had a frosty, determined look, the lips were compressed, the little chin was out, and the hands were clasped together tight before her. The curious cap on her head and the flash of white down the front of her uniform made her seem like some tiny, ruffled, white-breasted bird.

"You left them in Mr. Schofield's study," she said. Her voice was unnaturally, deliberately polite. "On top of the green filing cabinet in his study, sir, when you happened to go in there by yourself before dinner."

It took a few moments for the full meaning of her words to penetrate, and in the silence that followed I became aware of Mike and how he was slowly drawing himself up in his chair, and the color coming to his face, and the eyes opening wide, and the curl of the mouth, and the dangerous little patch of whiteness beginning to spread around the area of the nostrils.

"Now, Michael!" his wife said. "Keep calm now, Michael, dear! Keep calm!"

—Roald Dahl

He creates prize-winning wines with
the care a sculptor devotes to his marble.

Anonymous

6

Crossroads

Everybody from American Canyon to past Calistoga is proud of the fact they're from Napa Valley. My dad came over from Petaluma when he was in fifth grade; now he's seventy-five, so my family has lived in St. Helena for about sixty-five years. Dad and his partner, Jerry Garr, purchased Steves Hardware in 1953 from Warren Steves, who was the son of the original owner, J. H. Steves, who founded the store in 1878.

We're Italian. At first we thought maybe the name got chopped when my grandfather came through Ellis Island: the Italians pronounce it Menegoni, but it is Menegon. My grandparents owned about two acres on McCorkle Avenue near the Napa Valley Olive Oil Company. They lived in the main house, and they had a smaller house where we lived until I was eight or nine. My grandfather raised chickens and rabbits, and hc had a vegetable garden and a little vineyard—the federal government then allowed you to produce up to two hundred gallons of your own wine, I think. We'd make four or five fifty-gallon barrels of wine every year, most of it for our own consumption. Both those houses are still there, and they're my father's now.

Our roots are definitely planted here. Napa Valley is my home, the place where I'm raising my family—two boys and a daughter who's graduating this year from high school. My wife, Anne, is originally from England. She was living in San Jose, and would come up every other weekend to see her family in Santa Rosa. When my grandfather fell and broke his hip, my cousin Donna, Anne's best friend, would swing over the mountain to see him—and Anne used to come with her. One thing led to another, and we got married twenty-seven years ago. I count my lucky stars every day for her.

The quality of life in St. Helena is great. Growing up here in those days, the shops—what I can remember, anyway—tended to be more for the local St. Helena person. We had a sporting goods store and some little mom-and-pop drugstores. We still have Vasconi's, which I guess has been around forever, too.

The streets weren't as congested, and we played: we'd go to Crane Park and play our Little League baseball there, or we'd go on Sundays and play football out there on the lawn. We used to love going out in the wintertime—obviously it was wet and muddy, and we'd come home all muddied up and dirty. And my mom would say, "Clean up outside, don't come in the house!" During the winter we'd just ride our bikes up to the elementary school, which at that time had a basketball court that was not enclosed but that had a roof on it so we could play when it was raining. We would divide up teams, just like everybody would in those days—we'd divide up and play for hours. We didn't think of time, you know.

I was always active as a child and as a young person: sports is my big cup of tea. I love sports and I love being around kids, especially as I get older. I started coaching Little League when I was fifteen—as an assistant coach, strictly volunteer, as much a kid as some of my players—and I was promoted to the major league team, the Giants, which Steves Hardware sponsored then and now. I coached Little

League for thirty-plus years, and I was president for four years. Now I coach the high school girls' varsity basketball team. There are times when I'll tell my team, "You're tired today, but you need to push yourself. We need to set goals, and you need to try to accomplish them, and you need to try to think down the road." But in all sports—I don't care what age group it is—for the coach to do the job that he or she needs to do, I think you need to bring in what real life will be like. Kids have changed, and if you don't change and try to keep pace with them, they'll run right past you, they're learning so quick. So the love of sport, the love of competition, and just being around these kids on a daily basis kind of keeps me young.

The two things that I've enjoyed the most in life are running my own business, being a hardware person, and coaching. I get to do both, and sometimes I feel guilty about it—but you've got to do what you love doing. My brother Gary and I own the business with my mom and dad. My wife and brother work here, and I still consult with my dad. He's been a little bit under the weather the last couple of years, but he's definitely somebody we can talk to and get advice from. My mom, Louise, also works three days a week. All of my kids have worked here. It's still family, so it's rewarding, and we've made a lot of good friends.

—Ron Menegon

CARL DOUMANI

I was born and raised in Los Angeles. There was only the city proper of Los Angeles then, in 1932. There were still trolley cars, there were farms on the west side, and there was the riding trail down the center of Sunset Boulevard. My first job was cutting and edging lawns for a buck apiece. From age eleven on I worked, and I always enjoyed it. It was part of my upbringing.

When I got to UCLA, I worked at Dude's, a Texas pit barbecue and beer joint. I ended up buying half the business when I was twenty-one. I've always liked business. I like deals, and I like putting something together. I like building things, dreaming them up, and making them happen. I was in business school, but doing business was more fun, so I never finished, I never got my degree.

I was thirty-eight years old when I came up here. Joe McNeill, a family friend, brought my wife and me up to Napa Valley for a long weekend. We had a really nice time, so we decided to come back and try to find some little piece of land and put up a cabin so we and our four kids could vacation here.

Our broker, Ned Smith, kept telling me about Stags Leap, a four-hundred-acre property with an old winery and some other buildings. I wouldn't even look at it. I didn't want four hundred acres, and I didn't want a winery. One day he drove me in and said, "I just want to show you something." I'll never forget seeing the property for the first time. We stood on the porch of the old manor house, just looking out there. I was hooked, so we bought it. I didn't know anything about growing grapes or about making wine. I didn't know anything about anything.

In 1970 people in Napa Valley were leery of anybody who came from the outside, especially if you came from southern California. Acceptance took time. Instead of mailing the checks for the bills, you learned to go down to Knight Lumber, say, or Steves Hardware, and take the check with you. All the places you were buying products from, you went by, you let them see you, you were there. It took a while because they didn't think you were going to be around, and they didn't want to waste their time. These were the people who lived here, who had been born here, and we needed their help.

Napa Valley is a farming community. It's a different way of life. That's the big thing that you forget when you're from Los Angeles. When you're born and raised in the city, and you move into a community like this, you don't understand that you have to help each other, because nobody can cover it all.

When we first moved here, Bob Mondavi came over and introduced himself. He said, "We know the grapes on this property to be of really good quality, and we'd like to buy grapes from you." He also said, "Someday you're probably going to restore that winery. When you do, please feel free to come to us. We may not be able to tell you what to do, but we can tell you what not to do. Our people are there for you." And it was true: every year they would buy some new piece of equipment, and whatever they learned from it they passed on to anybody who was interested.

One day Lee Stewart of Souverain Winery was moaning that he had just lost his source of Chenin Blanc. I had Chenin Blanc, but Lee needed five tons. I went to Bob Mondavi—we had made a contract for the grapes—and asked him if he could spare the Chenin Blanc for Lee. Mondavi said yes. That was it, no question. I sold Lee the grapes, and we never discussed price. A month later, a check came for more than the going rate for Chenin Blanc. There was just your word, and it held.

Today we're part of the community, and we've got friends who share our concern for the valley. We're farming organically now, because we think it's the thing to do to take care of the land. We want to leave the land in better condition than we found it. For a long time, with all the chemicals and pesticides and stuff that we were using, we were killing the soil. Now there are more growers who are improving their farming practices, growing more organically, trying to resuscitate the soil. That's the stewardship, that's the thing that you hope you can do and get your neighbors to do.

I think in our final year at Stags Leap, we made fifty-five to sixty thousand cases of wine, which is a nice business. But I didn't want to run that kind of business. We finally sold it, and I came over here, to Quixote, to do what I really wanted to do, which was to run a much smaller winery. I'm sure Quixote represents something in my personality. Any time you create a business, or you build a building, or make a product, it's not an impersonal thing. It's got to have your personality in it. I've been called a quixotic character in the past. I've tilted at my share of windmills—and I hope to continue to do so.

— Carl Doumani

My role as an artist is not to identify

my own taste and my own aesthetic but to

find the aesthetic of the place.

Robert Irwin, Artist

7
The Valley

One of the greatest things that I do as a teacher is take kids to perform in Europe. I've done seven trips. This summer we're going to Spain to give concerts in Madrid, Valencia, Barcelona, and San Sebastián. We've sung at the Montreux Jazz Festival, the North Sea Jazz Festival in Holland, and the Vienne Jazz Festival in France, as well as in various city centers all over Europe.

I'm the choral director for the school district, so I teach kids from the fourth grade through the twelfth grade. On average, I teach three hundred fifty to four hundred kids every day. I don't know all their names, but I do know all their voices. The youngest are eight and nine. I have two choirs at the middle school, plus a little vocal jazz group that meets at lunchtime twice a week. At the high school, I have a morning choir, the jazz choir, and the Wednesday night girls' chorus of kids from the area who want to sing. I also have an after-school children's chorus, and the St. Helena Chamber Choir, an adult group that meets every Monday night. So I have about seven or eight choral groups that I work with within this community, plus the church choir, just to fill up my days.

Some of the school programs already existed when I started here thirty years ago, but I added four and started the chamber choir. I just jumped in and started teaching music. I had a small group of kids here, and then more kids and more kids got involved. I don't really let kids sing solos unless they can do it well. I don't just throw them up there and say, "Hey, go sing a solo because it'll be good for you." I don't want them to do that. I want them to sing when they really have something to offer, because that's when they really grow.

The kids are building a community of friends right here, in this room, every day. We make certain agreements before we get started: to share, to be an active listener, to be open, honest, respectful, compassionate, accepting—no put-downs. I try to teach those things to my kids every day. When they start to have a little bit of arrogance I jump all over them. If I sense that that kind of attitude is starting to seep into the group, I'll sit them all down and say, "Let's talk about how grateful you are for what you have—most schools are not able to have what you guys have."

Because I start them in fourth grade, and because most of them stick with me until they graduate, I watch them grow up. We become such good friends that they stay in touch with me after they leave school. Alums always come back for the concerts. A lot of my early students' children are in my program today—a lot. I would say that most of the kids now in my jazz choir I've taught their parents at one time or another.

My three daughters all went to school here, and they all sang in the choir. Angela is twenty-nine, and she teaches here at the primary school; Melissa is studying to be a music teacher; she's twenty-five. My third daughter, Carly, is twenty-two, and she's going into law for some reason.

I met my wife, Carolyn, at the College of Marin, in the choir. She was studying music, and got her degree in music, like I did. We went through school together: we were always in the same groups, the same ensembles, and then I got drafted into the Vietnam deal. The second year I was in the Navy, she joined me and we got married. I never went to Vietnam. I don't know why, I just lucked out. We didn't start our family until we moved to St. Helena, and we'd already been married seven years by then—now Carolyn teaches right across the hall from our daughter.

My wife and I go to a choral camp in the Berkshires every few years, and I still go to classes every summer. That helps me with my skills, and when I come back I can be a better teacher for the kids. You never reach the point where you're there. You're never there.

Sometimes I ask myself, how long can I keep doing this? If I'm not physically able to do it, if I'm not giving the kids the same spirit that I've given them since I started teaching, or if the intensity and passion start to lag, I'll quit just like that. Kids pick up on that, and I would never do that to these kids. I don't know any other way to do it. It's so rewarding, especially when the kids write me and tell me how much it meant to them and what they've learned through music. Most teachers don't have a clue the impact they have on students, but I've got dozens of letters and e-mails from mine. They all blow me away!

— Craig Bond

6/10/03

Craig,

My eighth grade year life should have been fun and easy; it was nothing even close to that. My grades weren't too bad but they were the worst to date, I had gotten in trouble for drinking with the school, and I was making one of the harder decisions in my life. That decision was about where I would be spending the next 4 years of my life. I weighed out the possibilities and the pros and cons of St. Helena and Thacher down in Ojai California, and my heart was set on Thacher. There was one thing though, and it kept me from signing the final paper. First the feeling started small and slowly grew like an anchor pulling a ship back to shore. As the feeling grew I began to recognize it more and more. The fact of the matter is, I wanted to sing with you for my remaining 4 years in St. Helena. This feeling overwhelmed me and I knew that staying in St. Helena, despite the lame crowd, was the choice I needed to make. I stayed at St. Helena High to sing in your choir.

After 5 years with you and 8 more before that just watching you with the choirs I knew that's what I wanted to do. Hell, I even remember the day when I sang along side your daughters and you came up to me after the show and said, "Douglas, you were magnificent, you're going to be in my choir someday." Well I grew up a bit, got into school and I was in and on my way and I just want to say that every step along the way was a pleasure.

Music has opened up a whole new world for me today, a world that I get lost in, and love it. That world is my band. Since four out of five of us are "choir boys" your influence is more than evident in our sweet harmonies and rockin melodies. Through you I was able to sing, and perform and right now in my life these things are what make me happiest.

Now we are coming to the end of our 9 year singer/director, teacher/student, friend/friend relationship and this is just one way that I'd like to say thanks. Thanks for making St. Helena worth it.

With love always,
Your devoted fellow tenor and captain,

Doug Streblow

STATION 17

TYPE OF ALARM	LOCATION
MEDICAL AID	
RESCUE	
STRUCTURE	
VEHICLE	
ACCIDENT	
GRASS OR BRUSH	
UNKNOWN	

THE VOLUNTEER

In the Fire Service, you earn being called Chief. You can be hired and get the title, but you still have to earn it—you have to get to the point where the guys trust you with their lives. My nine years as a volunteer here helped a lot, but I've also always been a leader, the captain of the team. Some of it is just God-given ability, but when I get involved in something, it's not a half-assed deal.

I've learned over the years that you can over-commit yourself, so right now I've got my family, I've got the fire department, I've got my business, and I've got the swim team. My daughter was born here, in St. Helena Hospital, in 1989, three years after we moved here. I ended up here because a friend of mine from college had moved here and my sister was teaching elementary school in Calistoga. This was after I was in the service, went to college, started a landscaping business, sold the business to my brother, moved to Nevada, and worked on a ranch for four and a half years—it's the longest I've been anywhere since I was a kid.

Either you're good in an emergency, or you're not. The camaraderie and adrenaline drive you, and the thing about firefighting is that every day you affect somebody's life positively. About ten years ago one of the most progressive chiefs in the United States, a guy named Alan Brunacini, from the Phoenix Fire Department—we call him Yoda—said, "We've built all these fire stations, and closed our doors. We're not part of the community anymore." We don't have that problem here: if somebody has a flood in the basement, we go pump the water out. We do whatever we can, go the extra mile. A few years ago there was a fire in a business on Main Street. It was Friday night, and a storm was coming. We searched and found a sober roofer on a Friday night, and we got the roof sheeted over before it poured. That business owner still thinks I walk on water. But we couldn't leave his roof open—that's being part of the community.

I've owned Whiting Nursery since 1986. I have my degree in plant horticulture from Cal Poly, and I know trees and shrubs. I landscaped for many years and taught classes in horticulture, so I've got a ton of plant knowledge—it's been kind of a natural, and it's connected me with everybody in town. When I heard about the nursery being for sale, my dad was dying, so it was months before I called David Whiting and learned that he and his wife, Margaret, were looking to retire. We met in late February 1986. I moved here in May, worked with him for two months, and then took over in July—and I kept the name because he had such a good reputation and was such a good plantsman.

I'm the oldest of five. I've got two sisters and two brothers. One of my younger brothers started playing Little League and I started coaching him, and I've coached ever since. I'm in good shape for a fifty-three-year-old, and I work out six days a week. If I don't get a workout there's something wrong, my body can feel it—you get addicted to your endorphins. So I swim three days, I run, I ride a bike, I do a spin workout, and if there's a fire the night before, that makes it a little tougher. I started master's swimming at the local pool because for my fiftieth birthday I wanted to do an Olympic-distance triathlon, which is a one-mile swim, a twenty-four-mile bike ride, and a ten-k run. It was ugly, but I learned—I survived the race, and kept swimming. The second year, I blew out my Achilles, and so I started helping the coach. This year they didn't have a coach, and they asked me to do it; a couple of parents help me with the younger kids. We do all the exercises with the kids. You have to: that way they'll respect you. We're trying to teach them fitness, and swimming is something that they can carry with them the rest of their lives.

The kids here all know me. We go to their schools for fire department inspections—we bring the fire trucks there—they see us down here, and they see me at the nursery. Having the kids wave at me, and know who I am, and that I'm a positive fire chief, that I'm doing the right things, and that I've got a good little business, that all works for me. Who would want to be a fire chief anywhere else? When it's done here, it's done. People say, "Oh, you should run for mayor." Who needs to run for mayor! Hey, the mayor, he makes $460 a month and he pisses off half the people in town. Why would I change jobs? I got the best job in town!

—Kevin Twohey

AMANDA

I've always loved horses. When I turned six years old, my mom took me to this little place on the Silverado Trail, and I did vaulting—which is like gymnastics on a horse—for two years. That was to get my balance. And then I started taking lessons. With riding, it takes so much practice to do even one thing right, perfectly. Other than horses, volleyball is my favorite sport—I'm on the school volleyball team. Last year I was on the school soccer team, but this year horses are much more important. I'm the vice president of our school. I thought it would be cool to learn about leadership, and there were a lot of things I wanted to change.

I'm in eighth grade, and I'm very excited about starting high school next year. When I go to college I might want to go to Europe and get my degree in riding horses. But if I do that, then I need to be good enough to earn a living. Otherwise I might want to be an architect, or a lawyer—I'm really good at arguing.

My dad loves to travel; he always wants to go somewhere. During the summers he always says, "We have to go to Europe for three weeks." My brother and I just say, "No way!" Me, my mom, and my brother usually win, so we do go on family trips, but they're usually just for about a week. When I travel, I feel how lucky I am to have a house and a family that loves me and horses.

Every night we have dinner together. We're always silent at first, but then we start a family conversation and it's really fun. We all laugh, and we joke around a lot, and we tease my dad especially. My brother and I are really good friends. We never fought or anything. We've always played together, so now it's just that we talk a lot more.

I love it here in Napa Valley. I wouldn't want to grow up in a city because there's too much going on and too many people. Here, I know a lot of the community. The outdoors is a big part of my life, and most of my friends do sports and are outside a lot. At night we're on the computer and phone, but not during the day.

I like my life. I mean, there are always good things and bad things. Well, there's nothing really bad, really. It's just being a teenager. I guess the hardest thing so far is that I've lost a lot of people—my grandma and my grandpa. And at our barn there's a lot of breeding, and a lot of foals have died in birth. I don't have any desire to be a vet, though. I'd rather be out there riding—just like I'd never want to be a cheerleader, because I'd rather play the sport than root for the team.

My dad always tells me to think five years ahead. Just like when we play games (our family plays a lot of games), he always tells me to think five steps ahead. And I do because he taught me to—in chess, and Chinese checkers, and Scrabble.

The horse world is a whole different world: there's a lot of competition, but there's also a lot of friendship, and I get a lot of support from my family. Right now, I'm at the perfect spot with my horses. When I turn fifteen, I'm going with a member of the American Olympic Team to Germany to find a horse—a really good horse—and then I'm going to try out for the Junior American Team. One day, hopefully, I'll get to the Olympics.

—Amanda

ALEX

It's really hard to play any sport with your parents, because no matter how much you love them, or how well you get along with them, there will always be some way to get in an argument. It becomes too competitive—especially with my dad, especially when we're playing golf or tennis. When we play golf, which is a love-hate sport that I usually hate, we always keep score, and I tend to get really mad, which leads to club throwing, which I try to refrain from doing. When I play tennis with my dad, though, I play more competitively because I can beat him.

Eating is also a sport for me and my dad, but not a competitive one. A lot of my interest in food comes from traveling. We've been to some exotic places, and about once a year we'll go somewhere in Europe, usually to see my grandfather, who lives in Paris and Berlin. I've always been an adventurous eater. I've got friends who, like me, love to try everything, and I've got other friends who just eat spaghetti, and peanut butter and jelly—very selective eaters are one of my pet peeves.

We come to Napa for three-day weekends, usually, and we spend a lot of time here in the summer and on longer vacations from school. My family has been coming up here since before I was born, and they've been members of Meadowood that long, too. Some of my earliest memories are of playing with kids at the kid pool. We'd run around, or explore on the bridge over the creek, or swing on the swing set—and we'd go and catch frogs.

My first real job was this summer, when I helped Doug King, Meadowood's tennis coach, with the kids' program. I'd had a vegetable stand, and I'd washed cars for pocket money, but this was the first time I had to interview and give someone my Social Security number. The little ones, the beginners, were a challenge, because I had to be very patient, but it was really fun to see how they could improve. Some of the older kids were pretty good, so it was nice to get the ones who were having trouble and be able to help. I've worked with kids before because of the community service program at my school. This year we're teaching underprivileged kids in a San Francisco public school about stories—we talk about everything from plot to character and moral.

Looking back, the job interview wasn't all that difficult. I just acted like myself, and I wasn't too nervous. You do have to think ahead, though, so you can be truthful, I guess, and be yourself in an unfamiliar place or a new situation. It's much easier to tell the truth than to lie, although I just wrote an English paper—an argumentative one—on how lying can be good. Its main point was that sometimes lying can help and truth telling can hurt: would you rather have a lie bring a smile or the truth bring a tear? That's a hard question.

—Alex

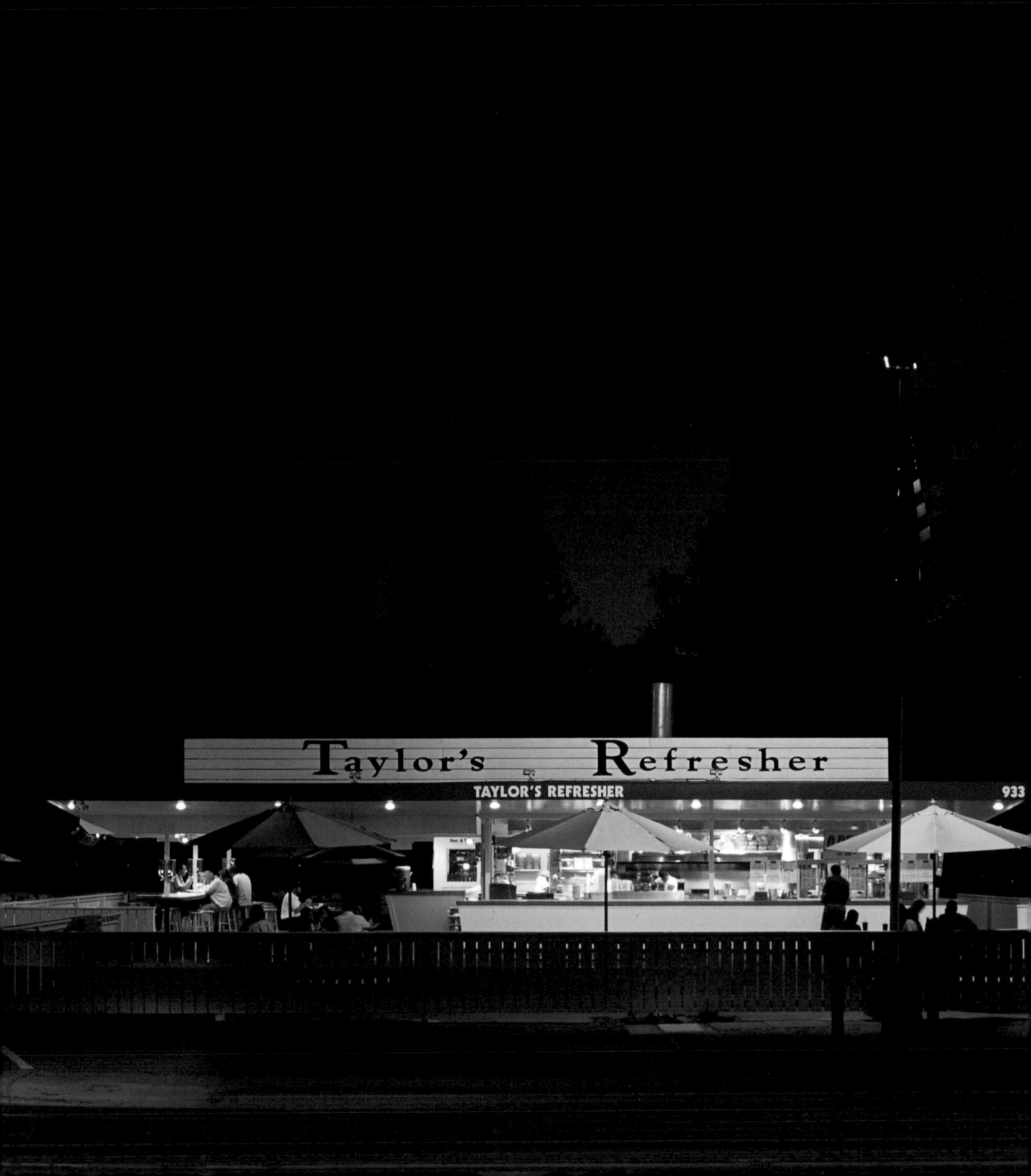
Taylor's Refresher
TAYLOR'S REFRESHER
933

8

The Natural

WINE, CULTURE
AND HERITAGE

*An Informal Conversation with Robin Lail
and Robert & Margrit Mondavi*

ROBIN LAIL: One of the fascinating things about the wine business is that even though people have been making wine for eight thousand years, there is still so much we don't know. I believe that the most important advances in our business have been made in the vineyard, and I think we still have a great deal more to learn in that arena.

ROBERT AND MARGRIT MONDAVI: Great wine is a traditional thing, but science has helped us to understand the art. For example, refrigeration was an incredible advancement because it allowed us to control the process of making white wine. We now know much more about farming and the appropriate time for picking grapes, etc. We have learned—and we continue to learn—about growing our grapes in the proper soil and climate. We have also learned what the subtle differences are between making good wine and making great wine. Yet even with all the new technologies and science, wine-making has remained virtually the same.

LAIL: We now see ourselves revisiting some age-old techniques, such as oak fermenters and basket presses. Granted, our current basket presses are automated and far more sophisticated than their ancestors, but they hark back to age-old techniques. So much technology has been added to our business in the last century. But when I think of the great wines that came out of Inglenook in its heyday, when things were extremely simple, I sometimes wonder what would occur if we experimented once again with head-pruned vines and simpler techniques.

MONDAVIS: Wine is culture. We realized early on that we would need to educate the American public about wine. Americans were not accustomed to drinking wine, unlike most families from Italy, France, Spain, and many other countries. We knew we would have to have patience in order to get results; we also realized that it would take at least ten years of consistent, hard work to get our wines accepted in the class of the world's top wines.

LAIL: Wine, at its best, is basically about people. It is about the stories and passions that drive people to immerse themselves in the pursuit of excellence and to contribute to making life a little more joyful for others. My most important contribution is to carry forward the family story into the twenty-first century—to continue to pursue the goals and passions brought by my great-grandfather Gustav Niebaum and my father, John Daniel Jr., and to pass them along to our children. History is always a stanchion in the progress of a community, and enthusiasm and commitment carry history into the present, and beyond.

MONDAVI: When my father and I discovered Napa Valley in the 1930s, it was immediately obvious to us that the combination of soil,

climate, and people here produced grapes that were truly exceptional. We knew that in the 19th century Napa Valley had had a reputation as a source of award-winning wines, a reputation built by pioneering immigrants like Jacob and Fritz Beringer, Gustav Niebaum, Jacob Schram, Charles Krug, and Hamilton Crabb. My father and I became part of a new wave of pioneers—Louis Martini, Andre Tchelistcheff, John Daniel, and others—who were starting to bring Napa Valley winemaking back to life after phylloxera and Prohibition. We wanted to make great wines with our own Napa Valley characteristics: wines that were gentle and friendly, that harmonized with food, and that had complexity, subtlety, and richness. So we talked to winemakers and universities to learn as much as we could about leading-edge technologies, and we took the science and the technology and blended it with the art of winemaking. The collegiality of the Napa vintners is well known: we shared our discoveries and worked in harmony with other Napa vintners then, and we still do.

LAIL: My father was a traditionalist through and through. From the time my sister and I were little girls, he spoke with us about the magnificence of Napa Valley and the beauty of the vineyards. I remember that on Sunday drives up and down the rows of vines, Dad would point to each varietal with the pride of a father and describe its individual virtues. There were long discussions about the family history and the hopes for the future of Napa Valley. There were probably genetic infusions that brought me into the wine business, and there were certainly environmental influences—walking home from school and stopping in at the winery for a glass of water, climbing the stairs to watch the wines fermenting in their open-topped fermenters, smelling the incredible heady aromas of harvest. In the spring, there was the joy of lying in the mustard and watching the clouds overhead, and looking for Indian arrowheads after the vineyards were plowed.

MONDAVI: I loved wine from the beginning, and I'll love it for the rest of my life. It was part of our family heritage. My mother was always in the kitchen, and she would give me a little wine in water with our meals. We learned early on that wine and food enhance the enjoyment of living. Isn't that something you would want to pass on to your descendants? My family has chosen to appreciate wine and participate in the business in a way that is similar to the choice my father and I made. I realize now that this comes from my Italian roots. My children and grandchildren are American, but they are proud of the fact that we are Italian, and they're proud of the contribution that Italy has made to world culture.

LAIL: I was a child of the vineyard. When Inglenook was sold in 1964 due to family differences, I was sad. But the thrill of what had been done and my curiosity about what more could be done fermented quietly over the years. Eventually it resulted in my inescapable desire to return to the business and to attempt to carry the heritage forward. The decision was not optional. It was a must, both a love affair and a way of life.

MONDAVIS: We have always believed in education. Since we started the winery in 1966, we have developed programs to heighten awareness of fine wine, food, and the arts, and we've devoted years to

233

researching wine's role in civilization. We are committed to sharing our passion for all good things in life. You have to educate people and invite them to have an understanding: that's why we founded COPIA. Margrit taught me that art plays an important role in enhancing the quality of life, right along with wine and food. She has created many arts programs here, and that's why we have always taught the concept of wine, food, and the arts together: with wine and art, food becomes a celebration.

LAIL: The world of wine is ever changing. It is filled with people on a quest. The bright future of Napa Valley can only be guaranteed by vintners who continue to search, who are fascinated with wine and passionate about it. For us here, preservation of the land that gives us our superb fruit is of the utmost importance. We must always remember that we are only as good as our most current vintage and that we are always in the debt of our vineyards. I believe the community of Napa Valley is unique in the world—and it's based on our shared vision, our respect for our land, our strong sense of community, and our undying fascination with the challenge of possible perfection.

MONDAVIS: Whatever you choose to do, you must make a commitment to excel, and then pour yourself into it with your heart and soul and complete dedication. Interest is not enough. If future generations believe in these simple principles, Napa Valley will continue to be the best it can be.

NOTES ON CONSERVATION:

THE NAPA RIVER WATERSHED

In the Napa River watershed, agriculture has long been king. The remarkable bounty of this incredibly fruitful land has supported everything from the field crops, cattle grazing, and timber production of the 1840s to the vineyards of today, which first developed in the 1860s. By the late 1960s, as demand for Napa Valley wines began to grow, vineyards began a rapid ascent toward becoming the valley's dominant form of agriculture. In fact, grape production in the Napa River basin has more than tripled in less than thirty years, from approximately fourteen thousand acres in 1968 to thirty-two thousand acres by 1989 to more than forty-three thousand acres in 2003.

Success often comes at a cost. In the case of Napa Valley, the price of the area's late-twentieth-century agricultural growth was not readily apparent for almost a generation. By 1990, though, increasing evidence of widespread erosion and the decline of steelhead trout resulted in the listing of the Napa River as "impaired" by sediment under the Federal Clean Water Act. This designation was a wake-up call to the community. It indicated that the very quality of life that had attracted so many to the region—and that was so highly valued—was now at considerable risk. It also signaled that the time had come to take action and begin the difficult task ahead, one that, if accomplished, would be a major achievement: restoring the health of the Napa River.

The community has spent the last decade laying a strong foundation for reaching that remarkable goal. Now the time has arrived to pursue a vision for the future of the Napa River watershed. First, some fundamental background on the setting: the Napa River watershed encompasses a basin measuring four hundred twenty-six square miles (two hundred seventy thousand acres). It ranges from five to fifteen miles wide, spans a length of forty miles, and climbs up to four thousand feet in elevation. The watershed also contains more than fifteen hundred miles of streams that flow from Mt. St. Helena into San Pablo Bay at the northern end of San Francisco Bay.

More than sixty-five hundred acres of valley floor wetlands have been drained and filled since the nineteenth century. Approximately twenty thousand acres of the watershed are currently covered by the impervious surfaces of pavement and rooftops, and more than forty-three thousand acres have been developed to cultivate agriculture. As recently as the late 1960s, local sanitation districts, tanning factories, and slaughterhouses all discharged their wastes—including raw sewage, heavy metals, and other toxins—directly into the Napa River.

The effects of such carelessness are measurable in a variety of terms, including the size of indigenous wildlife populations. The steelhead trout runs, for example, which had surpassed more than six thousand in the early part of the twentieth century, were decimated by years of pollution: the runs of one thousand to two thousand fish common in the late 1960s have been reduced to only several hundred fish at present. Chinook salmon also had a large and variable run until

239

the era of the Great Depression; their current population numbers are unknown. Coho salmon, once numbering two thousand to four thousand, were wiped out by the late 1960s.

While the abundance of native species has declined as the valley's population has grown and its agriculture evolved, the Napa River and its tributaries still continue to support a diverse and almost entirely intact community of sixteen native fish species—a level of diversity that remains unsurpassed in Central Valley and Sierra streams, and is matched by few Bay Area streams. Napa County, in fact, is one of the country's richest regions in terms of biodiversity, with up to 35 percent of the more than eleven hundred native plant species estimated to be rare and/or endangered.

Since the 1860s, Napa Valley has had twenty-seven major floods; in the last thirty-six years alone, floods have caused $542 million in damage. In 1998, voter approval of the so-called "living river plan" marked the beginning of a new environmental restoration approach to flood protection, reconnecting the river to its historical floodplain, maintaining fish and wildlife habitats, and restoring over six hundred acres of tidal wetlands. Indeed, more than one hundred thirty-five thousand acres of Napa County land is protected through public, quasi-public, and private ownership. That total includes thirty-three thousand acres protected by the Land Trust of Napa County in conservation easements or fee title.

The challenge today is how to meet the competing needs of the present—to balance agriculture, development, and conservation—

without compromising the ability to meet the needs of future generations. This is a daunting task, but one clearly within reach for a community with the strength of will to have made the Napa Valley what it is today.

We now stand at the crossroads to the future. The legacy that this generation leaves to the next, and to those that follow, still remains to be determined. If the community is to protect the very quality of life that it holds so dear, then it first must find a way to join together to envision a future that balances its many needs, that encourages stewardship of the land, that promotes sustainability, and that creates a shared sense of place that can be proudly passed from one generation to the next. It's up to the community to build on the strong foundation that already exists, and to take the next steps to make that vision of the future a reality.

—Rone Patrick Lowe Jr.
Deputy planning director of the
Conservation, Development & Planning
Department of Napa County

JOHN MUIR, 1964, IN FOREST OF REDWOODS
This stamp honored the great naturalist and conservationist
whose efforts helped save California's giant sequoias.

NATURE

To go into solitude, a man needs to retire as much from his chamber as from society. I am not solitary whilst I read and write, though nobody is with me. But if a man would be alone, let him look at the stars. The rays that come from those heavenly worlds will separate between him and what he touches. One might think the atmosphere was made transparent with this design, to give man, in the heavenly bodies, the perpetual presence of the sublime. Seen in the streets of cities, how great they are! If the stars should appear one night in a thousand years, how would men believe and adore; and preserve for many generations the remembrance of the city of God which has been shown! But every night come out these envoys of beauty, and light the universe with their admonishing smile.

The stars awaken a certain reverence, because though always present, they are inaccessible; but all natural objects make a kindred impression, when the mind is open to their influence. Nature never wears a mean appearance. Neither does the wisest man extort her secret, and lose his curiosity by finding out all her perfection. Nature never became a toy to a wise spirit. The flowers, the animals, the mountains, reflected the wisdom of his best hour, as much as they had delighted the simplicity of his childhood.

When we speak of nature in this manner, we have a distinct but most poetical sense in the mind. We mean the integrity of impression made by manifold natural objects. It is this which distinguishes the stick of timber of the wood-cutter from the tree of the poet. The charming landscape which I saw this morning is indubitably made up of some twenty or thirty farms. Miller owns this field, Locke that, and Manning the woodland beyond. But none of them owns the landscape. There is a property in the horizon which no man has but he whose eye can integrate all the parts, that is, the poet. This is the best part of these men's farms, yet to this their warranty-deeds give no title.

To speak truly, few adult persons can see nature. Most persons do not see the sun. At least they have a very superficial seeing. The sun illuminates only the eye of the man, but shines into the eye and the heart of the child. The lover of nature is he whose inward and outward senses are still truly adjusted to each other; who has retained the spirit of infancy even into the era of manhood. His intercourse with heaven and earth becomes part of his daily food. In the presence of nature a wild delight runs through the man, in spite of real sorrows. Nature says,—he is my creature, and maugre all his impertinent griefs, he shall be glad with me. Not the sun or the summer alone, but every hour and season yields its tribute of delight; for every hour and change corresponds to and authorizes a different state of the mind, from breathless noon to grimmest midnight. Nature is a setting that fits equally well a comic or a mourning piece. In good health, the air is a cordial of incredible virtue. Crossing a bare common, in snow puddles, at twilight, under a clouded sky, without having in my thoughts any occurrence of special good fortune, I have enjoyed a perfect exhilaration. I am glad to the brink of fear. In the woods, too, a man casts off his years, as the snake his slough, and at what period soever of life is always a child. In the woods is perpetual youth. Within these plantations of God, a decorum and sanctity reign, a perennial festival is dressed, and the guest sees not how he should tire of them in a thousand years. In the woods, we return to reason and faith. There I feel that nothing can befall me in life,—no disgrace, no calamity (leaving me my eyes) which nature cannot repair. Standing on the bare ground,—my head bathed by the blithe air and uplifted into infinite space,—all mean egotism vanishes. I become a transparent eyeball; I am nothing; I see all; the currents of the Universal Being circulate through me; I am part or parcel of God. The name of the nearest friend sounds then foreign and accidental: to be brothers, to be acquaintances, master or servant, is then a trifle and a disturbance. I am the lover of uncontained and immortal beauty. In the wilderness, I find something more dear and connate than in streets or villages. In the tranquil landscape, and especially in the distant line of the horizon, man beholds somewhat as beautiful as his own nature.

The greatest delight which the fields and woods minister is the suggestion of an occult relation between man and the vegetable. I am not alone and unacknowledged. They nod to me, and I to them. The waving of the boughs in the storm is new to me and old. It takes me by surprise, and yet is not unknown. Its effect is like that of a higher thought or a better emotion coming over me, when I deemed I was thinking justly or doing right.

Yet it is certain that the power to produce this delight does not reside in nature, but in man, or in harmony of both. It is necessary to use these pleasures with great temperance. For nature is not always tricked in holiday attire, but the same scene which yesterday breathed perfume and glittered as for the frolic of the nymphs is overspread with melancholy to-day. Nature always wears the colors of the spirit.

—from *Nature*
by Ralph Waldo Emerson, 1836

AFTERWORD

It has been said that there is a universe in life's little things, and that to grow, and to build something that lasts, one must slow down and look hard at what is at hand. When I moved to Napa Valley in the late 1970s, I was seeking something essential: a way of life with roots that feed a deeper satisfaction of permanence and fulfillment. For me it happened in the vineyards, where one begins to understand the cycles of life from the ground up.

A life of farming cultivates many things, including humility. Nature can be extremely capricious. It teaches one never to take bounty of any kind for granted. Anyone who grows something, even if it's just herbs on a windowsill or tomatoes in the backyard, knows this to be true.

Those who work every day in the democracy of the soil quite literally plunge their hands into the history of place, and of human effort itself. That is why names, and place names in particular, have meaning. Napa, Yountville, Oakville, Rutherford, St. Helena, and Calistoga—the names alone—connect those here now to those here before and to those who will follow.

From century to century, in Napa Valley as elsewhere, the refinement of human purpose and the growth of human knowledge and experience lead to continual improvements in the way that people use their land, and what those variations represent. There is a parcel of land east of St. Helena between the Napa River and the foothills of Howell Mountain that typifies this process. Over the last 200 years, the parcel has passed through the hands of General Vallejo to his niece Maria Soberanes; then, with

California's statehood, it passed to John Howell; at the turn of the twenti-eth century, the Marolf family purchased it, and farmed it for almost one hundred years. In these two centuries the use of that land has gone from wilderness to ranch to farm to vineyards. Now the process of its evolution has shifted slightly, yet again, to include, in addition to its vineyards, the fruit orchards, olive groves, apiaries, and kitchen and cutting gardens that, throughout history, have distinguished the self-sustaining estate.

Resolution may be honed here to a finer point than elsewhere. The transformation over centuries from wilderness to fine winegrowing estate reflects a notion of progress that includes respect for the places and the traditions that our forebears have bequeathed to us. This type of progress has ethical and cultural imperatives, in addition to the manifest pleasures of living well.

The goal as we move into the future is not only to continue to improve our land and the quality of what we grow but also to remain sensitive to the environment and the aesthetic of Napa Valley. The unique gifts of our culture and our countryside come with unique responsibilities. My hope is that we accept the duties that accompany our great good fortune, and that we manage the region's economics, environmental health, and social pressures with equal deftness.

Stewardship demands that we find a viable means for continuing the cycle of life in Napa Valley, and for easing its transition to the next century. History continues to remind us that the grandeur of human aspirations is always made modest by nature's majesty. And yet we persist. Each generation is, after all, another beginning.

—H. W. H.

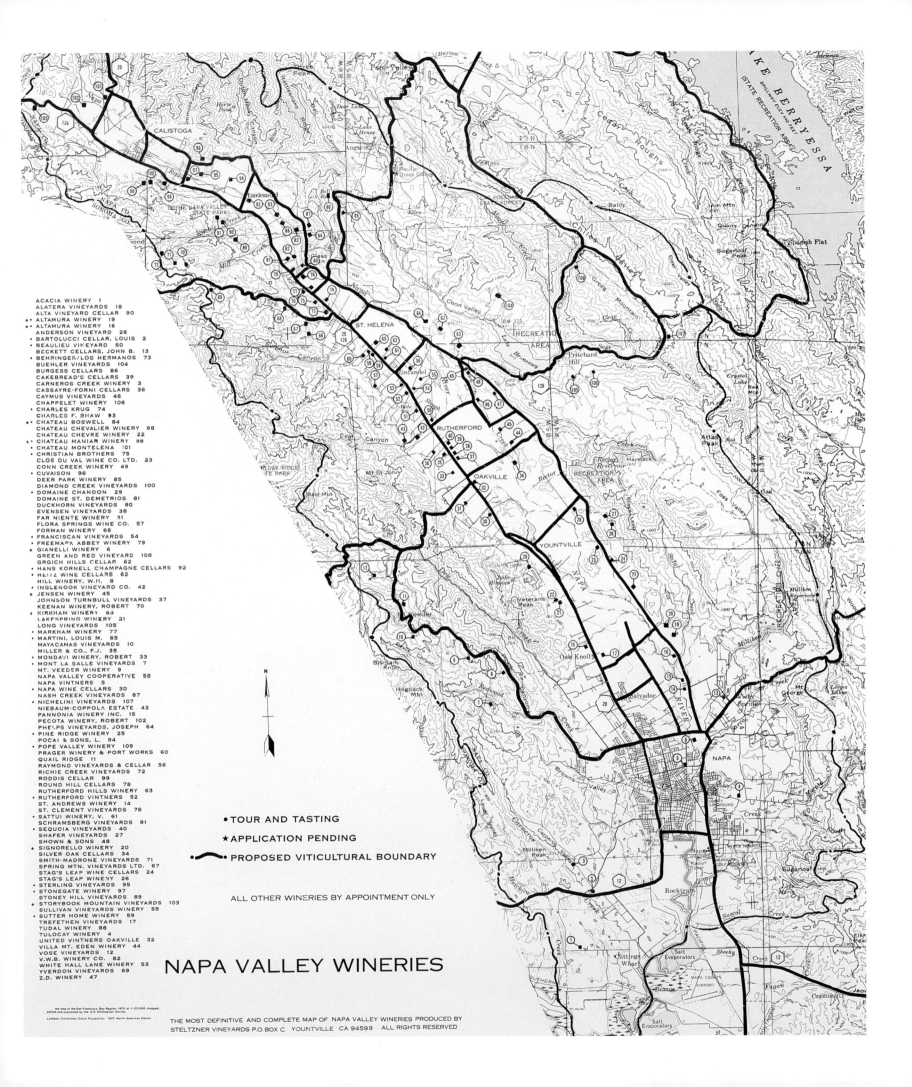

NAPA VALLEY WINERIES

INDEX OF PHOTOGRAPHY

REPRODUCTION CREDITS

Every attempt has been made to locate the copyright holders for the photographs and articles printed in this book. We sincerely regret any omissions.

Reproduction Credits:
Pages 46-47: Photograph of collage © 2005 D. James Dee; Marolf family photographs, courtesy the Marolf family. Little girl with bunches of grapes, 1923, photo © A. J. Winkler, courtesy Department of Special Collections, University of California, Davis. Jacki Stocker and Yonni Afman, © Cherri Lynn, courtesy Jacki Stocker.

Page 72: Courtesy the permanent collection of the Napa Valley Museum

Page 74: Courtesy Mr. Maurice E. Nayrolles/H. W. Harlan

Page 76 (left to right): *Coastal Miwoks Paddling*, c. 1916, by Louis Choris, courtesy Bancroft Library, University of California, Berkeley; *Mission San Francisco Solano de Sonoma*, c. 1885, by Oriana Weatherbee Day, courtesy de Young Museum, San Francisco, California, gift of Mrs. Eleanor Martin; General Mariano Vallejo with daughters and granddaughters, courtesy Bancroft Library, University of California, Berkeley

Page 77 (left to right): *Native Californians Lassoing a Bear*, c. 1873, courtesy Bancroft Library, University of California, Berkeley; *Vaquero*, c. 1830, by James Walker, Mrs. Reginald F. Walker collection, courtesy Bancroft Library, University of California, Berkeley; Bale Mill, courtesy Napa Valley Wine Library Association

Page 78 (left to right): *Peter Storm and the Bear Flag*, courtesy Sharpsteen Museum Association, Calistoga, California; *Joseph Sharp with Pick Axe in Hand*, courtesy Bancroft Library, University of California, Berkeley; portrait of Sam Brannan, courtesy David and Kathleen Kernberger

Page 79: Courtesy Napa Valley Wine Library Association

Page 80 (left to right): White Sulphur Springs, photo © R. E. Wood, courtesy David and Kathleen Kernberger; map of St. Helena, 1881, courtesy The Napa Valley Reserve; photo from the Marolf family collection, c. 1930, courtesy the Marolf family

Page 81 (left to right): E. J. Buena Vista Vineyard, filling and recorking sparkling wine, c. 1872-73, photo © Eadweard Muybridge, courtesy Bancroft Library, University of California, Berkeley; cover of *Up and Down California in 1860-1864, The Journal of William H. Brewer*, University of California Press, Berkeley, Third Edition, 1966, Edited by Francis Farquhar, © 1949 The Regents of the University of California; Jacob Schram and Charles Carpy, courtesy Schramsberg

Page 82 (left to right): Southern Pacific railroad car 1161, St. Helena Depot, c. 1867, courtesy the permanent collection of the Napa Valley Museum; Shuck Chan and family, Napa, California, courtesy the permanent collection of the Napa Valley Museum; *St. Helena Star*, Main Street, St. Helena, California, courtesy Napa Valley Wine Library Association

Page 83 (left to right): Jacob and Frederick Beringer, c. 1870-76, courtesy Beringer Vineyards; St. Helena Hospital, courtesy St. Helena Hospital; Gustave Niebaum, courtesy Wine Institute, San Francisco, California

Page 84 (left to right): Fanny Osbourne, courtesy Robert Louis Stevenson Silverado Museum, St. Helena, California; Italian Swiss Colony wine label, courtesy Wine Institute, San Francisco, California; Hannah Weinberger on her 80th birthday, 1920, photo © E. F. Cooper, Elite Studio, St. Helena, California

Page 85 (left to right): Tiburcio Parrott, c. 1885, courtesy the permanent collection of the Napa Valley Museum; Greystone, c. 1889-1900, courtesy Culinary Institute of America; Aetna Springs, courtesy David and Kathleen Kernberger

Page 86: Putah Creek Bridge, courtesy the permanent collection of the Napa Valley Museum

Page 87 (left to right): Champagne Eclipse promotional card, courtesy Unzelman Collection, Santa Rosa, California; woman sorting rootstock for grafting, courtesy Department of Special Collections, University of California, Davis; Pope Street Bridge, c. 1902, photo © E. F. Cooper, Elite Studio, St. Helena, California, courtesy David and Kathleen Kernberger

Page 88 (left to right): Ferry disembarking, courtesy the permanent collection of the Napa Valley Museum; Revere House Hotel (built in 1856), Napa, California, 1906, photo © M. H. Strong, courtesy David and Kathleen Kernberger; fruit pickers, Carneros, California, courtesy David and Kathleen Kernberger

Page 89 (left to right): Vintage Festival float, 1913, courtesy David and Kathleen Kernberger; Michael Heitz, (son) Jack P., and Louise Heitz enjoy a last drink before closing their winery at Prohibition, c. 1920, courtesy Gary Heitz/the permanent collection of the Napa Valley Museum; John Daniel Jr., courtesy Robin Lail

Page 90 (left to right): Crowds outside Beringer Vineyards as it opens for public tours, c. 1933, courtesy Beringer Vineyards; Brother Timothy Diener, F. S. C (Fratres Scholarum Christianarum), c. 1935, courtesy Brothers of the Christian Schools De La Salle Institute; Madame Fernande de Latour and Andre Tchelistcheff at Beaulieu Vineyards, c. 1930, courtesy Beaulieu Vineyards

Page 91: Farmer with rake, c. 1920, photo © E. F. Cooper, Elite Studio, courtesy David and Kathleen Kernberger

Page 92 (left to right): Carole Lombard at Beringer Brothers Winery, c. 1941, courtesy Beringer Vineyards; publicity still from the motion picture *This Earth Is Mine*, 1959, courtesy Napa Valley Wine Library Association; Taylor's Refresher, c. 1955-60, courtesy Joel Gott

Page 93 (left to right): M. F. K. Fisher, courtesy Napa Valley Wine Library Association; trademark twenty-mule team of the U. S. Borax Corporation, 1957, photo © Ralph Crane/Stringer/Getty Images, collection Time & Life Pictures; Robert Mondavi, c. 1960, courtesy Robert Mondavi

Page 94 (left to right): Aerial view of the Napa River, 2004, photo © Steven Rothfeld; in the Napa vineyards at harvest, courtesy the permanent collection of the Napa Valley Museum; Lisa Van de Water in the cellar at Mondavi, 1975, photo © Earl Roberge, courtesy Lisa Van de Water

Page 95: Robert Mondavi in the Mondavi barrel room, c. 1970, courtesy Robert Mondavi

Page 96 (left to right): Chateau Montelena 1973 Chardonnay label, courtesy Chateau Montelena; Chef Jeanty and staff, courtesy Domaine Chandon; Cathy Corison, c. 1978, courtesy Cathy Corison

Page 97 (left to right): Chappellet family members at the gala opening of Meadowood Napa Valley, 1979, courtesy Molly Chappellet; the first Napa Valley Wine Auction, 1981, courtesy Napa Valley Vintners Association; Ceja family members, photo © Rebecca Pronchick, courtesy Ceja Vineyards

Page 98 (left to right): Pro-Am Croquet Tournament at Meadowood Napa Valley, 1987, courtesy Robin Lail; cover of *The French Laundry Cookbook*, © 1999 by Thomas Keller, used by permission of Artisan, a division of Workman Publishing Company, Inc., New York. All rights reserved. Wine Auction gala at Meadowood Napa Valley, 2000, courtesy the Napa Valley Vintners Association

Page 99 (left to right): Robert Mondavi, Margrit Mondavi, and Julia Child at The American Center for Food, Wine, and the Arts—COPIA, 2001, © M. J. Wickman, courtesy COPIA; view of Meadowood Napa Valley from the croquet lawn, 2004, © Steven Rothfeld, courtesy Meadowood Napa Valley; view of The Napa Valley Reserve looking south, across the vineyard and towards Old Howell Mountain Road, 2004, © Steven Rothfeld, courtesy The Napa Valley Reserve

Page 100: Portrait of Robert Louis Stevenson, c. 1880, courtesy Robert Louis Stevenson Silverado Museum, St. Helena, California

Page 143: Detail of watercolor, © 1982, by Wick Knaus, courtesy Meadowood Napa Valley

Page 144: Detail of watercolor, © 1982, by Wick Knaus, courtesy Meadowood Napa Valley

Page 257: Map of the Napa Valley wineries, © 1977, Richard Steltzner, courtesy Steltzner Vineyards

The outer wrapper of this publication is a reproduction of *The Vintage in California—At Work at the Presses*, by Paul Frenzeny, from the original wood engraving, c. 1878, courtesy Bancroft Library, University of California, Berkeley

In the Shade of the Vines

Meadowood Napa Valley
900 Meadowood Lane
St. Helena, California 94574
Telephone 800-458-8080
Telephone 707-963-3646
www.meadowood.com

Publication © 2005 Meadowood, Napa Valley

A Brief History of Napa Valley by Mary Trasko with Dan Miller and Judith Nasatir, © 2005 Meadowood Napa Valley

Interviews by Dan Miller and Judith Nasatir, 2003, © Meadowood Napa Valley

Visiting a Friend's Country Estate © 2004 Robert Becker

This Meadow and These Woods © 2004 Heather McIsaac

The Silverado Squatters by Robert Louis Stevenson, first published in 1883 by Chattus and Windus, London

Vineyard Transformations © 2004 Louisa Thomas Hargrave

Excerpt from *The Story of Wine in California* by M. F. K. Fisher © 1962, renewed 1990 by M. F. K. Fisher. Reprinted by permission of Lescher & Lescher, Ltd. All rights reserved.

Wine and the Appreciation of Life © 2004 Jay McInerney

Taste by Roald Dahl reprinted by permission of Alfred A. Knopf/David Higham Associates. All rights reserved. Previously published in *Someone Like You,* a collection of short stories, 1954

Wine, Culture, and Heritage © 2004 Robert Mondavi/Robin Lail

Notes on Conservation: The Napa River Watershed © 2004 by Rone Patrick Lowe Jr.; authored and contributed in his private capacity. All rights reserved.

Excerpt from *Selected Essays of Ralph Waldo Emerson* by Ralph Waldo Emerson, reprinted by permission of Penguin Group (USA) Inc. All rights reserved.

Meadowood Napa Valley Project Coordinators:
 Ann Marie Conover and Lisa Savano

Design and Editorial Direction: Dan Miller Design, New York

Photography: Steven Rothfeld © 2005 unless otherwise noted in reproduction credits

Publication Editor: Judith Nasatir

Copy Editor: Jim Cholakis

Printed and bound in Hong Kong

ISBN 0-9753389-0-0

Acknowledgments
This publication would not have been realized without the help of many people. First, I thank my partners of a quarter century, John Montgomery, Cathy Stocker, the late Peter Stocker, and their families, for their ideas, support, and confidence. Maurice Nayrolles for his leadership in taste, integrity, and the art of gracious hospitality. He was invaluable in bringing our vision to life. I would like to express my warmest gratitude to all the individuals, wineries, and institutions that provided historic background and images for this publication, in particular Randy Murphy, who generously shared material from the Napa Valley Museum, and David and Kathleen Kernberger, who provided images from their private collection. Many thanks to those who gave their insights on the valley's history, especially Jamie Davies, Nina Wemyss, and Margrit Biever Mondavi. We are indebted to John Thoreen of Meadowood's Wine Center for sharing his vast knowledge and providing so many suggestions for images and research. I would like to offer my special thanks to Dan Miller for his inspired design and editorial vision for this book and to Steven Rothfeld for his glorious photography and to Ann Marie Conover for her support and guidance of this project. In addition I would like to thank Judith Nasatir and Mary Trasko for all their hard work and insights; it has been a great pleasure working with them. I extend my thanks as well to my steadfast staff, to all the members of Meadowood, to the Napa Valley Vintners Association, and to the community that we all love so much and for which I have a deeply personal commitment.

H. W. H.